Curriculum Studies and Educational Planning

Denis Lawton

HODDER AND STOUGHTON

LONDON SYDNEY AUCKLAND TORONTO

British Library Cataloguing in Publication Data

Lawton, Denis
  Curriculum studies and educational planning
  (Studies in teaching and learning)
  1. Curriculum planning.
  I. Title.   2. Series
  375'.001   LB1570

ISBN 0 340 33281 6

First published 1983
Second impression 1984

Printed and bound in Great Britain for
Hodder and Stoughton Educational,
a division of Hodder and Stoughton Ltd,
Mill Road, Dunton Green, Sevenoaks, Kent,
by Richard Clay (The Chaucer Press) Ltd, Bungay, Suffolk

Typeset in 11 on 12pt Plantin (Linotron) by
Rowland Phototypesetting Ltd.

Contents

Studies in Teaching and Learning

The purpose of this series of short books on education is to make available readable, up-to-date views on educational issues and controversies. Its aim will be to provide teachers and students (and perhaps parents and governors) with a series of books which will introduce those educational topics which any intelligent and professional educationist ought to be familiar with. One of the criticisms levelled against 'teacher-education' is that there is so little agreement about what ground should be covered in courses at various levels; one assumption behind this series of texts is that there is a common core of knowledge and skills that all teachers need to be aware of, and the series is designed to map out this territory.

Although the major intention of the series is to provide general coverage, each volume will consist of more than a review of the relevant literature; the individual authors will be encouraged to give their own personal interpretation of the field and the way it is developing.

Preface

In 1973 *Social Change, Educational Theory and Curriculum Planning* was first published. It is now out of date in some respects, but rather than attempt to revise it, I felt it would be better to write a different book with an orientation more suited to the problems of the 1980s.

During the 1970s the curriculum was discussed in a number of countries, including the United Kingdom: the Callaghan speech at Ruskin College was followed by the 'Great Debate' on education, and curriculum was frequently mentioned. But the curriculum debate in England, as elsewhere, tended to be conducted at a very low level. Too much attention was paid to narrow utilitarian views of schooling; cuts in educational expenditure soon followed, and curriculum planning sometimes became associated with 'back to basics'.

The main purpose of this book is to look at education in a much broader way, using techniques of cultural analysis as a means of curriculum planning. The analysis highlights a number of contradictions in society and a number of defects in traditional curricula. For example, it suggests that the problems of young people growing up in a complex urban, industrial society have been seriously underestimated; schools have generally failed to take seriously the moral, social and political aspects of culture in curriculum planning.

A related concern of this book is to warn teachers against the technicist, 'efficiency' model of curriculum. The United Kingdom has not yet suffered the full horrors of 'behavioural objectives' or 'performance-based evaluation', but there are occasional danger signs, and secondary schools are dominated by external examinations to a ridiculous extent. The alternative proposed is an open curriculum planned according to methods of cultural analysis.

London, 1983   Denis Lawton

1 The Study of Curriculum: Definitions and Ideologies

Education . . . involves the initiation of others into worthwhile activities. . . . Science, mathematics, history, art, cooking and carpentry feature on the curriculum, not bingo, bridge and billiards.

R. S. Peters*

Definitions do not necessarily help understanding, but it is sometimes necessary to attempt to clarify meanings, especially where words are used in quite different ways in different contexts. There is a problem about the meaning of curriculum. Some languages do not even have a word for curriculum, and translators at international conferences are faced with a difficulty. In French, for example, 'curriculum' tends to be translated by the phrase *cours d'études* (course of studies) which often conveys quite the wrong flavour of meaning intended by the English writer. Many educationists who have 'curriculum' somewhere in their title find the word an embarrassment – more than once I have had to extricate myself from a situation in which it was assumed that I spent all of my professional life working on timetables!

That kind of misunderstanding does, in fact, illustrate, or at least get close to, one of the major ways of interpreting 'curriculum'. A narrow definition of curriculum would limit it to *content*, that is, subjects on the timetable and what is taught under each of those subject headings. At the other extreme, curriculum is used in a very wide sense to include not only what is taught, but how it is taught and why. This would include curriculum evaluation, control and classroom interaction.

Most of the standard definitions of curriculum can be placed on this continuum which at one extreme limits curriculum to the content of what is taught, and at the other extreme would seem to

* (1966) *Ethics and Education*.

include the whole of educational studies. Elizabeth Maccia (1965) defined curriculum as 'presented instructional content'. Somewhat further along the continuum is Jack Kerr's (1968) definition: 'all the learning which is planned and guided by school, whether it is carried on in groups or individually, inside or outside school'. Some would regard this definition as very wide indeed, but others would still object to its narrowness; one view of the 'hidden curriculum' would be that it is precisely that part of the curriculum which is not planned and guided by the school, but simply happens.

It seems to me useful to make a distinction between curriculum which is planned and other kinds of learning which are either accidental, unplanned, or may be even quite undesirable. Jim MacDonald (1971) suggests that it is necessary to have an agreed working definition, and accuses curriculum development experts of irresponsibility in their writing when they define curriculum as anything broader than 'a plan for instruction'. I would be willing to accept that limitation (although there are difficulties about the use of the word 'instruction' which we will encounter later in this book) provided that it were understood that the term 'curriculum *studies*' is necessarily concerned with much more than plans for instruction. Curriculum studies will involve a whole range of discussions about content, justification for that content, the translation of plan into practice by teachers, the reception of those plans and so on. In order to deal with those difficult issues it will be necessary to draw upon aspects of the disciplines of philosophy, sociology, psychology and history.

It may also be useful at this stage to make a distinction between curriculum studies and curriculum development or curriculum reform. If the terms are used synonymously, then the field of curriculum studies is being restricted to a very narrow range of issues, and also assumptions are being made about the desirability of change which ought to be examined rather than taken for granted. At a later stage I would also want to suggest that a very useful way of looking at the curriculum and at curriculum studies is to define curriculum as 'a selection from a culture'. If curriculum is a plan for instruction, then defining curriculum as a selection from a culture widens the range of curriculum studies to include justification as well as evaluation.

More important perhaps than questions about whether curriculum is used in a wide or a narrow sense, is the ideology behind any definition of curriculum. It is impossible to discuss curriculum in

a meaningful way without first establishing some kind of 'philosophy' of education including discussion of the values involved. The
content of education is necessarily dependent on what we think
education is for as well as for whom it is intended. I will eventually
make my own 'value' position clear, but first we should establish
certain basic premises.

I have already pointed out that there is a difference between
curriculum studies and curriculum development, although they
are often used as if they were synonymous; similarly, curriculum
theory and curriculum planning overlap but are by no means the
same process. Curriculum is also an interesting example of an area
where theory does not necessarily precede practice. Curriculum
development takes place, for a variety of motives, when individuals or groups – especially teachers and others concerned with
the planning of curricula – are dissatisfied with what is being
taught or with the methods employed in classrooms. The science
curricula in the USA and UK in the 1950s provided some good
examples of this kind of change. Educationists looked at the
results obtained by existing curricula and indicated their dissatisfaction – perhaps because the programmes were inefficient or out
of date – and proceeded to set to work on improving them. The
result in the USA, for example, was a series of science curriculum
projects funded by a federal agency which became known as the
'National Science Foundation'.[1] In the UK, Nuffield Science
Projects followed similar directions, but on a much more modest
scale. When teachers or professional curriculum developers
attempted to improve the curriculum (or sections of the curriculum), they came up against a number of difficult questions. In the
case of science, for example:

'Why teach science anyway?'
'Should all children learn science? If so, why?'
'If so, what kind of science?'
'What is science?'
'What is school science?'

These kinds of questions do not necessarily all arise at the same
time, but those concerned with curriculum development in any
subject area sooner or later find themselves asking questions
which are 'theoretical' issues. Curriculum studies is, therefore,
different from curriculum development which is only part of a
much wider set of curriculum issues that are partly historical,
partly philosophical, sociological and psychological. In this sense,
curriculum studies is parasitic upon what are often regarded as the

foundation disciplines in education,[2] but in other respects, curriculum studies asks different kinds of questions or at least approaches the questions from a different point of view. It is not always helpful to begin curriculum studies by assuming that development or reform is the first priority. It may be much more important to establish the total context of the curriculum by asking fundamental questions about it rather than taking it for granted, or trying to improve the teaching of it.

Similarly, it might be argued that curriculum theory should precede curriculum planning, but in practice this is not usually what happens. If we distinguish curriculum planning from curriculum development by saying that curriculum planning is concerned with the whole curriculum (rather than just a part as, for example, with a curriculum development project in science), then it would seem to be sensible to base a plan on some kind of theory – just as a plan for a bridge might be based on certain principles of engineering and physics – but even here we should perhaps remember that bridges were built long before engineers and physicists got involved. In education, what often happens is that someone is given the task of planning or replanning a curriculum, who may be not even fully aware of his or her own educational 'theory'. If asked, that person might even deny having a theory, preferring to be seen – like so many practitioners – as a sound practical teacher. But just as any teacher has a theory whether or not he or she realises it, so an educational planner faces choices and takes decisions on the basis of some kind of value or set of values which are the basis of a theoretical position. Every statement that a teacher makes in a classroom is value-laden, connected with ideas about the purpose of education, perhaps even the purpose of life. And so it is for educational planners and curriculum developers.

Those curriculum developers in the 1950s who were concerned with revising science curricula occasionally claimed that they were 'value-free'. But they soon had to face questions about the purpose of school science: was the major purpose really to provide enough scientists for industry and particularly war-time industry? Or was the purpose of school science to equip *all* young people with an understanding of one very significant aspect of their social and physical environment? It is impossible to answer that kind of question without bringing values into play.

Teachers and educational administrators as well as politicians all operate with some kind of 'social theory' in the sense of sets of assumptions, value positions, and ideas about the purpose of society. These views may, however, lack coherence, and some assumptions may contradict others. One important purpose of curriculum studies is to clarify issues and questions, to relate points of view to more general ideologies and to make clear what the theoretical choices are. Curriculum studies is therefore concerned with theories rather than with a curriculum theory. In this sense curriculum studies might have some similarity to studying politics. No one would expect a university course in political science to conclude by telling the graduates how to vote at the next election; this book will not have a final chapter saying exactly what the curriculum should include, but it is hoped that in both cases the choices will be clearer and the basis of decision-making established according to rational principles.[3]

My colleague Malcolm Skilbeck (1976) has suggested that there are at least three basic educational ideologies each of which generates a different type of curriculum theory:

1 classical humanism;
2 progressivism;
3 reconstructionism.

These ideologies are, of course, 'ideal types' in the sense that they rarely, if ever, exist in a pure form – most individual teachers might easily find themselves in at least two of the camps. But this may be where the danger of incoherence lies – some aspects of one ideology may be quite incompatible with beliefs appropriate to one of the other ideologies.

One of the interesting, perhaps distressing, features of schools is how similar they are in all societies despite differences in ideology.[4] This may be connected with a fourth ideology: what Skilbeck refers to as the 'technocratic-bureaucratic ideology' that lies behind a good deal of contemporary discussion of education, including ideas about assessment, testing and evaluation.

Classical Humanism

Classical humanism is probably the oldest educational ideology, originating in Greece in the fourth century BC when Plato developed the idea of cultural heritage, whose custodians were a class of 'guardians'. The ideology survived the Middle Ages and the Renaissance, and was put forward again in modified forms by

Matthew Arnold (1869) and by T. S. Eliot (1948). An essential feature of classical humanist ideology is that it associates tradition-al culture and values with a small minority group – 'the elite'.[5] This elite was referred to by Plato as the 'men of gold' who were to receive a quite different education from the other two 'lesser metal' groups. A clearly outlined twentieth century version of this view is that of Professor Geoffrey Bantock, who has written frequently about two types of education for two quite different classes of the community: he refers to a literary education for a small minority and the need to have a quite different 'popular culture' education for the masses based on an oral tradition.[6]

According to Plato, only a very small elite was to have the freedom to pursue enquiry and even for them only after a commit-ment to the values of the state had been thoroughly inculcated. Much of what Plato advocated in *The Republic* and *The Laws* might now be regarded as indoctrination rather than education. This charge could not, however, be levelled against Professor Bantock. Bantock advocates two forms of schooling which would accept the irreconcilable differences between 'high culture' and mass culture. Bantock's motive would appear to be social and cultural rather than, as with Plato, mainly political. Bantock is less concerned with the stability of the state than with providing each section of society with a worthwhile education. He thus advocates for the masses – not very carefully defined, but presumably including the working classes and the lower middle classes – a wide range of activities based on folk culture rather than high culture. His reason for this recommendation is not that a high culture education would be dangerous for the masses, but simply that they would not or could not benefit from it. Their traditional culture is so different, according to Bantock, that it is impossible to make high culture or literary culture available to them. What must be done, therefore, is to devise a combination of movement studies and moral education which they can understand and benefit from, and which would also be in some sense 'worthwhile'. It will be necessary for us to return to this theme of the Bantock view of an alternative education to classical humanism. At this stage, how-ever, we are more concerned with the characteristics of classical humanist curriculum.

A classical humanist curriculum would concentrate on cultural heritage; those kinds of knowledge which have been worked out over hundreds of years as giving access to the best in terms of literature, music, history and more recently, science. The development of the classical humanist curriculum could be traced historically through the medieval trivium and quadrivium to the idea of the Renaissance man, and then to the nineteenth century public school and Oxford or Cambridge educated Christian gentleman. Certain subjects which were regarded as high status and character training were the curricular goals.

The main reason why classical humanism can no longer be acceptable as an ideology in most societies is that it runs directly counter to democratic ideals of social justice and equality of opportunity. In most democratic societies education is regarded both as a means of encouraging greater equality, and as a 'good end' in its own right which ought to be available to all rather than confined to a small elite. An additional reason for its non-acceptability is more practical: the relevance of what has traditionally been regarded as the high status forms of cultural heritage is increasingly questionable. The kind of subject-matter suitable as a 'badge of rank' for a nineteenth century gentleman even when modified to some extent and brought up to date, is hardly likely to have general educational appeal.

It may be important, however, to make a distinction between rejecting the classical humanist ideology because it is essentially anti-democratic, and rejecting either the idea of cultural heritage or the importance of subjects and subject-matter. It will be a part of my later argument to establish the importance of 'cultural heritage', somewhat differently defined, for all young people, not simply for the future leaders of societies.

Progressivism

Progressivism, or child-centred education, also has a long history. The 'bible' of progressivist ideology is Jean-Jacques Rousseau's *Emile* (1762). Whereas classical humanism is 'knowledge-centred', progressivism is child-centred and represents a romantic rejection of traditional approaches to education. More important than transmitting a cultural heritage is the need for the child to discover for himself and follow his own impulses. An essential aspect of Rousseau's ideology was that childhood is an important period in its own right and should not be regarded as preparation for adulthood. Freedom was more important than social order.

The tradition was made into a more specific educational programme by such figures as Pestalozzi and Froebel, whose influence is by no means without importance today in teacher education.

The tradition has also survived in the twentieth century in a variety of forms: one extreme form was advocated by A. S. Neill;[7] a somewhat less extreme version was put forward by R. F. MacKenzie;[8] and a modified progressivism at one point seemed to become the accepted official view of primary education in the UK on the appearance of the Plowden Report with the child-centred title *Children and their Primary Schools*.[9]

A curriculum based on progressivism would be concerned not with subjects, but with experiences, topics chosen by the pupils and 'discovery'. Knowledge in the form of facts would be regarded as of very little importance, although acquisition of important concepts and generalisations might be given priority. Children's own writing and painting would be seen as of much greater value than appreciation of cultural heritage. In its most extreme form the curriculum would be that of the romantic individualists, rejecting traditional knowledge and values completely, in favour of the young discovering their own way of life.

The difficulty about accepting 'progressivism' in its entirety as an ideology is that it is based on an over-optimistic view of human nature. Rousseau and his followers assumed that individual human beings were 'naturally good' but tended to be corrupted by an evil society. Hence the doctrine of allowing children to choose a curriculum (or perhaps no curriculum) for themselves, and the importance of allowing children to develop without the harmful influence of society. But it is now very difficult to accept the notion of children being naturally virtuous; there is a good deal of evidence to demonstrate 'natural' selfishness which is only made tolerable by the influence of adults insisting on social conventions. A more acceptable view of the child-society relationship is that they are not in conflict: a child only becomes truly human by developing socially as well as individually. Children and society are complex mixtures of good and evil, and education consists to some extent of encouraging the good and trying to eliminate the evil in both.

Once again, however, to reject the ideology as a whole is not to dismiss all the beliefs and practices of progressive education. The child-centred ideology was, in many respects, a healthy reaction against the almost inhuman treatment of children practised in Rousseau's day and in the nineteenth century. In addition the stages of development approach, hinted at by Rousseau and others, has been advanced by Piaget as the basis of a much more scientific approach to children's learning. Finally, the motivational advantages of allowing children *some* choice is now clearly established.

Reconstructionism

If classical humanism is knowledge-centred, and progressivism is child-centred, reconstructionism might be regarded as society-centred. This would, however, be to over-simplify, since an essential aspect of reconstructionism would be to see the individual and society as harmoniously integrated rather than necessarily in opposition.

The essence of social reconstructionism is that education is seen as a way of improving society (and thus giving a better opportunity to the individual members of that society). In the USA, reconstructionism is often associated with John Dewey, for whom the experimental methods of science provided the most appropriate approach to social questions. This 'experimentalism', combined with his view of democracy, underlay much of Dewey's thinking about the relation between education and society. For Dewey democracy was not simply a form of government but a way of life which provided maximum opportunities for experimentation and growth. Education for all was, therefore, both a desirable aspect of democratic society as well as a means of achieving a better democracy. Above all, education was concerned with opportunities for the 'growth' of individuals within the modern industrial world. In this way the quality of life of individuals, and hence the quality of society itself, would continuously improve.

In the UK, reconstructionism might be associated with H. G. Wells and Bertrand Russell and, in the field of education, with Karl Mannheim.

Skilbeck (1976) summarises reconstructionist ideology as follows:

1 the claim that education can be one of the major forces for planned change in society;
2 the principle that educational processes should be distinguished from certain other social processes, such as political propaganda, commercial advertising, or mass entertainment, and that the former should, if necessary, enter into conflict with the latter in pursuit of worthwhile ends or goals;

3 the aspiration to make a new kind of person who would be better and more effective than the average citizen of today's society;

4 an interest in core curriculum in which prevailing social norms and practices are analysed, criticised, and reconstructed, according to rational democratic and communitarian values;

5 a conception of learning and the acquisition of knowledge as active, social processes, involving projects, problem-solving strategies guided, but not dominated, by teachers;

6 the elevation of teachers and other members of a carefully selected and highly trained elite of educators, who are designated the agents of cultural renewal;[10]

7 the relative neglect of difficulties and of countervailing forces – a characteristic feature of all kinds of Utopian thinking of which reconstructionism is 'one of the recognisable strands'.

It is important to note, however, that over-optimism and 'Utopianism' are features of *some* reconstructionists, but not essential characteristics of the 'ideology'. It is quite possible to believe that education can be used to improve individuals and society, without falling into the trap of thinking that there is somewhere an educational formula which would produce a perfect society or heaven on earth. Karl Popper (1945) has criticised Utopianism and its fallacies, and condemned it as a belief likely to lead to totalitarianism: to be a Utopian you have to *know* what is best, but anyone who knows what is best will eventually be tempted to impose what is best on the others whose views differ from his own. Utopianism might be classified as a very extreme version of social reconstructionism; it is also possible to see the two as quite different in their outcomes: the essential difference is that whereas Utopians have a very clear vision of the perfect society, social reconstructionists only see ways of improving society. It is quite possible to believe that education can be used to eliminate certain injustices, for example, without believing that education can make society perfect. For a reconstructionist, education can provide exactly the kind of piecemeal social engineering which was advocated by Popper (1945).

The reconstructionist curriculum would lay stress upon social values – in a democratic society, for example, citizenship and social co-operation; knowledge is not ignored, but a 'why' question is never far away, and knowledge for its own sake is highly questionable; knowledge is justified in terms of individuals' social needs, not in terms of custom, or cultural heritage *per se* (although cultural heritage may have considerable social importance under some circumstances). For these reasons, subjects will not be taken for granted to the same extent as in a classical humanist curriculum, and various patterns of 'integrated studies' or faculty structures will tend to assume more importance than subject departments in secondary schools. The kind of knowledge such as Latin and Greek traditionally seen as a badge of rank will be frowned upon, possibly being replaced by classical studies as part of an integrated humanities programme. Science and mathematics will be taught to all pupils, not because they are useful as a form of vocational preparation, but because these kinds of knowledge are important for an understanding of society. The curriculum will also be discussed in terms of a common culture and what all young people have a right of access to.

One tradition of reconstructionism has been strongly associated with the University of London Institute of Education. Sir Fred Clarke (1943) spoke of the renewal of culture through education; he acknowledged his debt to Karl Mannheim who was for a short time a professor at the Institute; Clarke's reconstructionism is epitomised in his phrase 'the educative society'. Although the 1944 Education Act has disappointed many educationists in its effects, its ideals were certainly reconstructionist in many respects. Education was seen partly as a way of combating Nazi and Fascist ideologies, partly as a way of improving the quality of life in the whole society. In the early post-war period this reconstructionist 'ideology' was strongly reflected in a document called *The Content of Education* (1945), which might have converted the ideals of the 1944 Act into a workable curriculum had it been taken up by Local Education Authorities (LEAs). *The Content of Education* was part of the Clarke-Mannheim-Institute of Education tradition; Professor Joseph Lauwerys, of the Institute, edited the report, which recommended a planned curriculum with a common core including the social sciences.

The view taken in the following chapters is a democratic, non-Utopian version of social reconstructionism. This is not to say that there is no value in the other two ideologies but that, given a democratic society which values certain kinds of freedom, the social reconstructionist ideology (or one particular version of it) is the most appropriate model. Progressivism and classical humanism do not stand up to an analysis of the needs of individuals growing up in twentieth century society, and therefore are inappropriate ideologies although aspects of their beliefs can certainly be incorporated into the social reconstructionist view. To be committed to an ideology such as reconstructionism (that is, improving education to improve society) is however only the first stage in deciding on a curriculum – as we shall see in the chapters which follow.

It is not, of course, the case that the three educational ideologies outlined in this chapter are the only ones possible. Reference has already been made, for example, to a bureaucratic-technicist ideology which has some links with utilitarianism. The three ideologies discussed, however, are readily identifiable in educational debates in the UK, USA and elsewhere.

It is also important not to ignore the relation between educational ideologies and deep-rooted social and political beliefs as well as psychological attitudes. Classical humanists, for example, tend to be associated with political conservatism. Other writers have pointed out the existence of fundamental differences in beliefs about 'human nature' which affect social and educational views: if you believe, with Hobbes (1588–1679), that human beings are essentially selfish, then not only will you reject progressive ideology but you will also be highly suspicious of any child-centred practices in education.

Since Skilbeck (1976) described the three educational ideologies, there has also been a good deal of dispute of a non-educational ideological nature which has, however, serious educational implications. In many western industrial societies in recent years economic debate has centred around the question of social planning versus the free market. This is clearly an ideological dispute stemming from social priorities and values. Those who favour planning will tend to support greater state provision and expenditure at all levels of education, whereas the advocates of 'the market' would want to minimise public expenditure on education and encourage parents and others to spend their own money – if they wished – on education or training for which they saw some clear benefit.

This kind of dispute, when it spills over into education tends to develop into a false opposition between justice and freedom. The ideological positions are, however, much more complex than that – as Rawls (1972), Dworkin (1977) and Ackerman (1980) have shown.[11] At a time of economic difficulty it is, however, easy for social justice in education to become a lower priority. The danger then is that of a retreat to a policy of classical humanist education for a small minority (probably those who can afford to pay), with basic elementary instruction plus vocational training for the majority.

Summary

Education cannot be value-free. Different value systems or ideologies will generate different curricula. In twentieth century democratic societies attempts are being made to educate all young people, whereas classical humanist ideology focuses on an elite minority. Progressivism as an ideology is rejected partly because its view of human nature is unrealistic, partly because it fails to relate curriculum to society or knowledge. Given a 'democratic' society which retains a number of undemocratic features, some kind of reconstructionist approach would seem to be necessary; reconstructionist ideology assumes that education can be used not simply for the benefit of individuals but also to improve an imperfect society. A reconstructionist curriculum will be a common curriculum based on a selection from the culture of a society.

NOTES

1   See Tanner and Tanner (1975) for an excellent summary of this period of curriculum development in the US.
2   Philosophy, psychology, sociology and history of education are sometimes referred to as the 'foundation' disciplines, to be distinguished presumably from 'teaching methods' for the various subjects and age-groups.
3   I am indebted to Mr Mike Golby, of Exeter University, for that comparison.
4   M. Stubbs (1976), for example, notes that 'teachers rarely ask questions because they want to know something . . . (This) question-answer pattern . . . has been found to have been stable over the past fifty years . . . and across different countries . . . although it has regularly been criticised by educational theorists' (page 90).
5   Matthew Arnold was very confused about the conflicting values of elitism and democracy. See Imelda Palmer (1979).
6   The most accessible version of this 'classical humanist' view of

'popular education' is contained in two articles for *The Times Educational Supplement* 12 March 1971, and 19 March 1971, reprinted in M. Golby *et al.* (1975).

7   A. S. Neill wrote a large number of books on 'progressive education' in the 1920s and 1930s based partly on his own school 'Summerhill'. His was probably one of the most extreme examples of the child-centred, anti-classical heritage approach: 'To write a bad limerick is better than to learn *Paradise Lost* by heart' (*The Problem Child*, page 178). I have criticised Neill's writing in some detail. See Lawton, D. (1977).

8   R. F. MacKenzie represents a less extreme version of progressivism in his book. See also Open University Course E203.

9   Despite the official acceptance of this view of progressive primary education, however, the majority of primary schools in England and Wales remained fairly traditional in terms of teaching methods. See, for example, Bennett, N. (1976).

10 Karl Mannheim's writing is particularly relevant to this view of the teaching profession. See, for example, Mannheim (1940).

11 The philosophical debate is a complex one, but one important aspect of it is to suggest that justice and freedom should not be seen as alternative goals but as complementary concerns in a democracy.

2 The Problem of Curriculum Objectives

For centuries . . . skilled craftsmen have been making metals. They have learned to add a little of this substance and a little of that, then heat the batch for a certain length of time until it reaches a certain colour, then let it cool at a certain rate. . . . Meanwhile 'scientific' approaches to metallurgy have not succeeded in fully explaining all that the master craftsman does. . . . Isn't it possible that teaching is at least as complex as metallurgy?

Myron Atkin*

Given that education is concerned with improving individuals, and indirectly with improving the society in which individuals live, there is still much disagreement about how to translate that general educational purpose into curricula. The problem is two-fold: first, what constitutes 'improvement', and second, what kind of curriculum planning model is most appropriate.

I want to start with the second of those problems which will lead naturally into the more fundamental question. During the last forty years or so, the most influential model in curriculum planning has probably been that of Ralph Tyler (1949), which has served to stimulate curriculum development all over the world in schools, higher education and in professional and vocational training courses of various kinds. Tyler (1949) begins by suggesting four fundamental questions to be answered in connection with any curriculum:

1 What educational purposes should the school seek to attain?
2 What educational experiences can be provided that are likely to attain these purposes?
3 How can these educational experiences be effectively organised?

* (1967–8) 'Research Styles', *Journal of Research in Science Teaching*, pages 338–9.

4 How can we determine whether these purposes are being attained?

These four questions are sometimes translated into a simple, linear model:

1 aims and objectives
↓
2 content
↓
3 organisation
↓
4 evaluation

It has been pointed out (Tanner and Tanner, 1975) that these four questions were by no means original, but we owe to Tyler the clarification of an approach which has become known as the Tyler rationale.

One objection to the curriculum model based on a four stage linear sequence is that it is far too simple. It is open to Bruner's suggestion, for example, that leaving evaluation until the final stage of the sequence is like doing military intelligence after the war is over: in other words, evaluation should take place at every stage. This would make the curriculum model (figure 1) a complex cyclical one rather than a simple linear progression. This may be more in keeping with Tyler's original thinking and this kind of model has been put forward and elaborated on by the Australian writer, Wheeler.

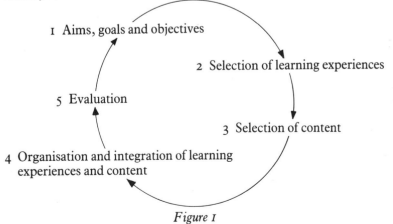

Figure 1

There are, however, more fundamental objectives to the Tyler rationale. Since the model has been of such importance for so long and continues to be influential more than thirty years later, I would like to look very carefully at its origins and only then proceed to an analysis of the criticisms which have been levelled against it.

Precursors of Tyler

The idea that a curriculum must be thought of in terms of objectives, which has been taken for granted by many curriculum workers, has had a relatively short history. Tanner and Tanner (1975) discuss an attempt thirty years before Tyler to use 'activity analysis' as an approach to curriculum planning:

> Developed by Franklin Bobbitt and W. W. Charters, the method activity analysis came to be cloaked as the scientific way to build a curriculum. According to Bobbitt, life consists of the performance of specific activities; if education is preparation for life, then it must prepare for these specific activities; these activities, however numerous, are definite and particularised, and can be taught; therefore, these activities will be the objectives of the curriculum.

> (page 27)

Curriculum building was, for Bobbitt, the job of an 'educational engineer' (Bobbitt, 1924). He was, in many respects, attempting to apply to education the industrial psychological techniques of the infamous F. W. (Speedy) Taylor. Those who criticised Ralph Tyler and the objective school for advocating an industrial or engineering model – treating human beings as if they were mere products to be run off an assembly line – were not entirely wrong.

Furthermore, the whole of the Bobbitt approach rested on an assumption that each area of 'life activity' did really consist of exactly specifiable components; but even if that were true and it had been possible to translate those components into curriculum, such educational engineering would have resulted in a completely static society. Tanner and Tanner (1975) and Callahan (1962) show that the efficiency movement in education was a reflection of a wider 'industrial' ideology.

Another aspect of the Bobbitt plan was that educational goals and standards should be set, not by teachers and educationists, but by businessmen. When Bobbitt applied the techniques of activity analysis and job analysis to curriculum construction, he estimated that what schools taught should be reduced to about 20,000 or 30,000 specific mechanical skills. It was, of course, a time when behaviourist psychology was also in vogue and this provided a further theoretical prop for the Bobbitt curriculum. Fortunately, the Bobbitt formula was not put to the test for very extensive periods: in the 1930s, Dewey and his followers became much more influential.

By the 1940s, however, the time appeared to be right in the USA for a swing of the pendulum to scientism[1] and the objectives approach to curriculum. Tyler's book in 1949 was enormously influential, but it is also important at this stage to distinguish between what Tyler himself wrote and what has been put forward by other curriculum theorists such as Mager and Popham, who have taken up much more extreme positions on the meaning of 'objectives'. R. F. Mager (1961), in his work on programmed learning, demanded that objectives should be specified operationally at definite levels of performance, and then extended his demand to cover any educational intents or goals:

> Curriculum objectives must always be pre-specified in terms of measureable changes in student behaviour.

Popham (1969), although sometimes appearing to disagree with some of Mager's excesses, also insisted on limiting the meaning of objectives to behavioural objectives. This narrow definition is related to Bobbitt's wish to see a clear separation between means and ends, between instruction and curriculum. The end (the curriculum) must always be clearly stated as a change in student behaviour.

It should also be noted that some other curriculum theorists such as Hilda Taba (1962) took a much wider view of the meaning of objectives, but by the early 1970s there was a powerful movement in the USA demanding that the only meaningful interpretation of objectives was to emphasise *behavioural* objectives, and numbers of educationists appeared at curriculum conferences with lapel badges and car stickers marked with such slogans as 'Help stamp out non-behavioural objectives!'

In fairness to Tyler himself, it must also be said that at a later stage (1973) he did return to the field to criticise some of the more extreme versions of his model – in particular, he lamented the failure by some educational leaders to 'distinguish between the learning of highly specific skills for limited job performance and the more generalised understanding, problem solving skills and other kinds of behavioural patterns that thoughtful teachers and educators seek to help students develop' (R. W. Tyler, 1973).

Several writers have put forward fundamental objections to the behavioural objectives approach and to the behaviourist psychology associated with it. It is perhaps remarkable that many of the curriculum theorists who spend so much time talking about objectives, tend to take existing objectives for granted rather than to submit them to critical scrutiny or even to ask where they come from. Thus, many so-called curriculum developers define their task as simply improving the efficiency of existing programmes rather than seeking to justify them or to revise them by a consideration of basic principles. Tyler himself falls into this category. Kliebard (1970) complained that Tyler's treatment of educational objectives was simply a *description* of the status quo when what was required was a critical analysis of the three sources of objectives, 'learners, contemporary life and subject specialists'. In other words, we are back to the situation I discussed towards the end of chapter 1, namely, being faced with three kinds of approaches – the child-centred, society-centred and knowledge-centred, but with no attempt being made to evaluate their *relative* importance or to judge specific inputs from any one source. The three-fold description is simply an acceptance of the educational status quo and an inadequate rationalisation of it in terms of 'sources'. Tyler accepts (1949, page 13) that curriculum inputs from the three sources have to be checked against an acceptable philosophy, but it is precisely that philosophy which is never made clear either by Tyler himself or by any of his followers. The criteria by which decisions are taken and choices made in terms of selecting some objectives and rejecting others are totally absent.

> To say that educational objectives are drawn from one's philosophy, in turn, is only to say that one must make choices about educational objectives in some way related to one's value structure. This is to say so little about the process of selecting objectives as to be virtually meaningless. One wonders whether the long-standing insistence by curriculum theorists that the first step in making a curriculum be the specification of objectives has any merit whatsoever.
>
> Kliebard (1970)

Another kind of attack on the behavioural objectives view has been put forward by Stenhouse and others. Stenhouse (1970), for example, was particularly opposed to the view that an objective should be stated in terms of students' behavioural change rather than in terms of an activity to be carried out by a teacher. Not only does the behavioural objectives view assume that teachers can always know exactly what response will be appropriate for every pupil in the class, but it also makes very doubtful assumptions about the nature of knowledge.

Reference has already been made to the engineering and industrial context of the behavioural objectives model, but it is also important to realise that much of the enthusiasm for the behavioural objectives approach derives from military training. Few would doubt that in training soldiers how to clean and strip a rifle, the behavioural objectives formula might be just what is required, but when the prespecified behavioural objectives approach is declared to be the *only* way of planning education of any kind, at any level, the problems begin to loom large. Stenhouse (1970) has pointed out, for example, the folly of attempting to list the behavioural changes in pupils which could be predicted as a result of their studying a Shakespearean play. Since every individual's response to a work of art is unique, then how could a teacher predict a correct response to a speech by Hamlet? Who could possibly state as a final judgment that Gielgud's interpretation was 'better' than Olivier's? In the arts an important objective, but certainly not a behavioural objective, is tolerance of ambiguity. The alternative is what Reid (1978) refers to as 'right answerism'. This is also related to another criticism of the behavioural objectives model, namely, that it encourages trivialisation – that if teachers have to prespecify and then test everything in their teaching programme, they will tend to emphasise all the most easily tested, but the least significant, aspects of any subject or topic.

In an effort to reconcile the merits of the behavioural objectives approach with the difficulties of applying the model to the whole of education, Elliott Eisner (1969) made an important distinction between what he called instructional objectives and expressive objectives. Whereas with instructional objectives a teacher must predict exactly what behavioural changes will take place if teaching is successful, in the case of expressive objectives there is no such certainty, nor would it be desirable:

An expressive objective describes an educational encounter. It identifies a situation in which children are to work, a problem with which they are to cope, a task in which they are to engage; but it does not specify what from that encounter, situation, problem, or task, they are to learn. An expressive objective provides both the teacher and the student with an invitation to explore, defer, or focus on issues that are of peculiar interest or import to the enquirer. An expressive objective is evocative rather than prescriptive.

Eisner (1969)

Eisner's distinction is a very helpful one, but I wonder whether the use of the word 'objective' in connection with the kind of expressive experiences Eisner refers to, might be a disadvantage. It may be confusing to use a word which has now acquired a certain precision in a way which may obscure the meaning once again. I would prefer Eisner's alternative terminology of educational *process*; in this way he is clearly contrasting the importance of the measurable product in the objectives model with the importance of educational encounters, processes or experiences involved in the more open-ended kinds of education. Eisner goes on to point out that the mode of evaluation in these expressive contexts is similar to aesthetic criticism:

. . . that this, the critic appraises a product, examines its qualities and import, but does not direct the artist towards the painting of a specific type of picture. The critic's subject matter is the work done – he does not prescribe a blue-print of its construction.

Eisner (1969)

In a later work, Eisner has extended this metaphor to consider evaluation as a kind of 'connoisseurship' (Eisner, 1975).

An equally strong objection may be levelled against behaviourism and behaviourist psychology. B. F. Skinner (1968) in a book appropriately entitled *The Technology of Teaching* not only reduces pupils to mechanical objects but also degrades teachers in the same way. Skinner describes the teacher's role as a purely mechanical one: the teacher is one who 'arranges the contingencies of reinforcement' by which pupils are automatically conditioned for specified behavioural changes. This mechanistic and atomistic view of human life is dangerously Utopian rather than reconstructionist. It is not helpful to discuss the education of human beings as if it were the same as the training of pigeons. Perhaps the most succinct attack on behaviourism was Chomsky's (1959)[2] review of Skinner.

It is also important to stress that the arguments against the behavioural model do not only concern the arts and what are often regarded as the more creative subjects of the curriculum. Some critics of behaviourism have been prepared to accept the model for such subjects as mathematics and physics whilst rejecting it for English literature, art and music. But this is too simple a distinction: the behaviourist model is just as unsuitable for the teaching of science for the following reasons. If science is not regarded as a collection of facts, but in the way that Popper has suggested as a series of hypotheses waiting to be refuted, then to teach science in the behavioural objectives way is to teach anti-science or non-science. According to Popper, the essence of scientific thinking is to realise that we *know* nothing for certain and that science is concerned to construct useful conjectural (and tentative) explanations. To give a very simple example, it was once reasonable to suggest (as a hypothesis) that 'all swans are white' – until a species of black swans was discovered in Australia. 'Swans are white' was a useful hypothesis or even helpful generalisation until it was refuted. But a science teacher who made his pupils learn 'all swans are white' (as a 'fact') was transmitting to his pupils an unscientific attitude. But this is precisely what the behavioural objectives model does for most, if not all, of the time. The teacher 'knows' and transmits 'the known facts' to the pupils who must memorise them.

The final objection to the objectives model is that teachers, perhaps especially good teachers, do not work that way – that is by using behavioural objectives. To that criticism Popham has replied that teachers ought to work that way, but it may well be that the teachers are right and Popham wrong! Stenhouse (1975), with greater respect for teachers and a better understanding of teaching and learning, makes the case for grounding curriculum study in the study of classrooms: 'rational curriculum planning must take account of the realities of classroom situations. It is not enough to be logical' (Stenhouse, 1975, page 75).

If we put all these criticisms of the behavioural objectives model into perspective it adds up to the conclusion that the mistake of behavioural theorists was to try and make the objectives model apply to the whole of the curriculum rather than to parts of it. Because the behavioural objectives model works splendidly for teaching typewriting, some theorists assumed that it would work equally well for all educational processes, and were misled by behaviourist psychologists into underestimating the complex nature of human learning. There is also more than a slight suspicion that the behavioural objectives model is related to an extremely narrow concept of education concerned with job-training and conformity rather than improving the quality of human life.

Having rejected the behavioural objectives model as a complete theory of curriculum, it will be the task of later chapters to construct another model within which behavioural objectives will play a limited part.

Summary

The behaviourist view of human beings, and the behavioural objectives model of curriculum have been examined and rejected. Both views are philosophically and psychologically unsound and anti-humanistic. The behavioural objectives approach can only be applied to certain kinds of low-level skills, not to the whole curriculum. The behavioural objectives view of curriculum is that of a closed system, whereas in a democracy individuals need to become autonomous by means of an open-ended curriculum. One of the purposes of the curriculum is to encourage 'tolerance of ambiguity' rather than 'knowing the right answers'.

NOTES

1 'Scientism' may be defined as the view that the inductive methods of the natural sciences provide the *only* possible source of knowledge about human beings and social questions; the fact that human beings think and reflect upon what is happening is ignored. Those like myself who wish to criticise this approach would label it as 'anti-humanistic', since it treats humans as though they were objects.

2 Chomsky's attack on Skinner is similar in many respects to the general criticism in Note 1 above. Chomsky points out that the human capacity for language is different *in kind* from, say, pigeons' ability to learn to play ping-pong. The relationship between language, thought and behaviour makes the study of human beings essentially different from either natural science or biology. See Chomsky (1959).

3 Curriculum Planning and Cultural Analysis

> Only in a quite limited sense does the single individual create out of himself the mode of speech and of thought we attribute to him. He speaks the language of his group; he thinks in the manner in which his group thinks.

Karl Mannheim*

A major difference between human behaviour and that of other animals is that we rely much less on instinct than on learning. Instead of knowing what to do instinctively, human beings have to learn appropriate behaviour patterns. A bird does not need to learn how to build a nest: that complex set of skills is innate, transmitted genetically. But humans do have to learn how to use tools, how to use language, how to know what is regarded by others as appropriate or inappropriate behaviour, as well as other aspects of their culture. The disadvantage of this is that children are dependent on adults for a long time during infancy and childhood; on the other hand, a significant advantage is that human behaviour is much more flexible or adaptive – we do not have to do exactly what our parents did, but can make improvements or changes of various kinds.

Definitions of culture

Raymond Williams (1976) has suggested that 'culture' is one of the most difficult words in the English language, partly because it has a history of shifting meanings, and partly because the word is now used to cover important concepts in several distinct disciplines and in several incompatible systems of thought.

* (1936) *Ideology and Utopia*, page 2.

The popular usage of culture tends to identify certain kinds of 'high' or minority taste culture – certain kinds of music, literature and art in particular, which are associated with the upper classes. When I refer to the curriculum as a 'selection from the culture of a society', I do not mean that the curriculum should be restricted in that way to 'high culture'. This would be inappropriate because the notion of high culture begs the whole question about what is important or worthwhile.

Culture as used by sociologists and anthropologists means everything that is man-made in a society: tools and technology, language and literature, music and art, science and mathematics, attitudes and values – in effect, the whole way of life of that society.[1]

> Culture is . . . that complex whole which includes knowledge, belief, art, morals, law, custom, and any other capabilities and habits acquired by man as a member of society.
>
> Tylor (1871)

> The sum total of the knowledge, attitudes and habitual behaviour patterns shared and transmitted by the members of a particular society.
>
> Linton (1940)

Any society has the 'problem' of transmitting its way of life, or 'culture', to the next generation. In simple societies culture is transmitted directly by the family or other 'face to face' interaction. In complex societies, the division of labour and social mobility make it impossible for culture to be passed on by traditional, informal means, and the task is partly entrusted to formal education.

Education is concerned with making available to the next generation what we regard as the most important aspects of culture. Because schools have limited time and resources, the curriculum should be planned carefully to ensure that an appropriate selection from culture is made. The selection should be neither arbitrary nor idiosyncratic. It should be open to rational enquiry and justification.

In order to plan a curriculum based on a reasonable or a justifiable selection from culture, however, it is necessary to have a process or set of principles by which it can be seen that the selection from the culture is made. That process will be referred to as 'cultural analysis'. The term cultural analysis may be used very loosely, both by those who simply wish to describe the relation between a society and its educational system, as well as by those who wish to prescribe certain necessary changes in curriculum (perhaps because education has lagged behind the 'needs of society', for example). What is nearly always lacking in discussions of curriculum, however, is any kind of systematic attempt to analyse the culture or cultures before a 'selection' is prescribed. What is often put forward as cultural analysis turns out to be no more than an individual, idiosyncratic judgment about the most important kinds of knowledge or the most worthwhile activities the schools ought to concentrate on.

The following is an attempt to outline a method of cultural analysis which can be argued and justified. It does not, of course, claim to be 'value-free', but it does attempt to state values explicitly. 'Justification' therefore takes place in a context of values, some of which might be societal values enshrined in legislation (such as 'equal opportunity' in many societies including the UK), others will be more basic human values common to all societies, and some may be values of a more controversial kind.

A good deal of work by social anthropologists has been carried out in the field of cultural analysis, but although this is of considerable importance as general background, very little can be applied directly to the task of cultural analysis for the purpose of curriculum planning. Social anthropologists, even when they are involved in cross-cultural studies, tend to be more concerned with fundamental aspects of society such as family and kinship structures rather than making links between, for example, economic institutions and knowledge systems. The classic cross-cultural studies which have been carried out by Murdock (1949) on social structure are methodologically interesting, but almost completely without relevance to studies of educational institutions. Even the work of R. B. Cattell (1949) which would seem to be relevant is only partly applicable to the task of cultural analysis in the field of education. Cattell set out to discover the primary dimensions of culture, and studied sixty-nine 'contemporary nations'; a vast programme of factor analysis led him to the strange conclusion that the six major dimensions were: size; cultural assertion (urbanisation); enlightened affluence; thoughtful industriousness; bourgeois philistinism; and cultural disintegration. These would be interesting points of comparison for certain kinds of society, but are a long way away from 'primary dimensions of culture'.

Cultural Analysis

There are basically two approaches to 'cultural analysis': the classificatory and the interpretative. The classificatory method would take us in the direction of check lists, tables and elaborate systems of classification. The interpretative method would be more concerned with looking at the culture as a whole.

Some anthropologists have attempted elaborate systems of classification of simple or 'less developed' societies by listing and categorising such key characteristics as kinship systems, economic features, religious beliefs, and so on. The danger in this approach is of being so concerned with the wealth of detail that it becomes impossible to make any generalisations at all. On the other hand, it is also possible that anthropologists may misinterpret a society by relying on their dominant impressions and reaching conclusions too readily.

The educationist attempting to analyse his own society has some advantages over an anthropologist in a less developed society – he is unlikely to be so completely misled as some anthropologists appear to have been by native informants – but he will also suffer from the disadvantage of looking at his own society through his own ideology or belief system. He will tend to take some aspects of culture for granted which ought to be questioned; he may assume the value of certain practices which ought to be examined; the power of tradition is particularly strong, not least in the field of education.

Part of the answer would seem to be that anyone attempting cultural analysis has to learn to stand back from society and attempt to see it, to some extent, as 'an outsider'. The observer attempting to analyse can never be 'value-free', but he can at least learn to become aware of his own values, beliefs and prejudices.

Measurement or Interpretation

Some aspects of culture can be measured (for example, some of the most important economic features in advanced industrial societies), but observers should beware of the temptation to measure what is easily quantifiable and then being dominated by these measurements. Cultural analysis is more complicated than manpower planning (and there is more to culture than work and training for work). Much of cultural analysis will be at the level of description, as the following statement indicates:

The concept of culture I espouse . . . is essentially a semiotic one. Believing, that man is an animal suspended in webs of significance he himself has spun, I take culture to be those webs and the analysis of it to be, therefore, not an experimental science in search of law, but an interpretative one in search of meaning.

Geertz (1975)[2]

In attempting to see how the curriculum in a society is derived from the unique culture of that society, it will sometimes be necessary to be more specific than the Geertz definition, and to ask detailed questions about knowledge, skills, values, and so on. But it will always be important to have at the back of one's mind that kind of interpretative view of culture. There will always be more to a culture than a list of its measurable features, and we will run the risk of over-simplification if we try to reduce a culture to tables and check-lists, although there may be times when tables and check-lists will have a limited use.

I am proposing, therefore, an eclectic system of cultural analysis which will make use of what is measurable when it is relevant, but will look for major categories and parameters within which to operate both quantitatively and interpretatively.

At the simplest level, cultural analysis when applied to curriculum planning would ask:

(a) What kind of society already exists?
(b) In what ways is it developing?
(c) How do its members appear to want it to develop?
(d) What kind of values and principles will be involved in deciding on (c) and on the educational means of achieving (c)?

Cultural analysis also involves asking questions about the extent to which a school system already matches the needs of society, as well as the kinds of curriculum change that will be necessary to achieve certain kinds of changes regarded as desirable.

In the process of cultural analysis it is always necessary to view culture as a historical as well as a contemporary process. An important aspect of analysis is not only to 'take a snapshot' of culture as it is now, but also to see how it has developed to that point. In educational analysis, it is also necessary to look out for culture lag and curriculum inertia: especially in rapidly changing societies there is a powerful tendency for schools to lag behind other aspects of social and cultural change, and for the curriculum to become increasingly irrelevant. This is not to fall into the trap of identifying 'educational needs' with 'technological advance' nor to equate education with vocational training: as we shall see, an adequate system of cultural analysis will demonstrate that education must be concerned with much more than technology and work; nevertheless, it is well established that in societies undergoing change, there is a tendency for curricula to become out of date unless conscious efforts are made to counter the natural[3] conservatism of teachers and schools.

Another difficulty is, of course, that sometimes schools will be right to lag behind certain changes in society (if society has moved in a 'wrong' direction, then schools and teachers may be right to wish to return to a previous stage).[4]

The essence of the cultural analysis approach is that of developing a method of matching the needs of individual children living in a specific society by means of a carefully planned curriculum. This selection from the culture is made by analysing the kind of society that exists, and then 'mapping out' the kind of knowledge and the kinds of experience that are most appropriate. This process requires three kinds of classification: first, deciding on major parameters (the cultural invariants); second, outlining a method of analysis which can be used to describe any given society, making use of those major parameters (that is, moving from cultural invariants to cultural variables); third, a means of classifying the educationally desirable knowledge and experiences. In the past a great deal of discussion has taken place about the classification of knowledge (for example, Hirst and Phenix)[5] but little attention has been paid to the task of describing accurately the kind of society that exists, and deriving from that analysis an account of the kinds of knowledge needed by the young at various stages of their intellectual development.

A diagrammatical outline of this approach, represented as a series of sequential stages, is set out in figure 2. As a model and, therefore, as a simplified version of reality it could be used at any level of curriculum planning: it could be used, for example, by a committee given the task of drawing up national guidelines for the curriculum; or at the level of school planning, by a curriculum committee to organise the curriculum into a timetable; or even by an individual teacher making his own choice of materials.

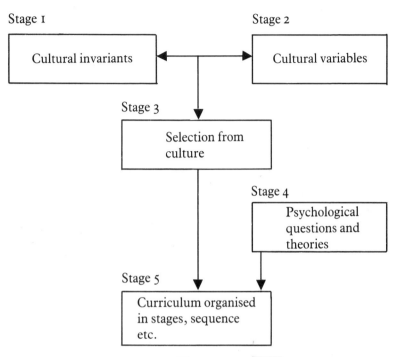

Figure 2

Stage 1: Cultural Invariants

Anthropologists such as Ruth Benedict (1934) have emphasised the differences between societies; others such as Clyde Kluckhohn (1949) and Dorothy Lee (1960) have stressed the essential similarities between all societies. Our purpose here is to begin by looking at the characteristics that all human beings appear to have in common (the human universals and cultural invariants) within the Kluckhohn and Lee tradition, and then to analyse how these are or should be related to educational processes.

In analysing cultures and cultural invariants to educational processes, I suggest that we should concentrate on eight major headings. It is not suggested, of course, that the eight parameters are exhaustive. It would be possible, for example, to say that all societies eat food, and then proceed to analyse societies according to diet. This might be interesting, but would not help us in the task of curriculum planning. Nor would it be helpful to classify societies according to family and kinship patterns using the Murdock techniques. Instead, I suggest that there are good anthropological and sociological reasons for sub-dividing the cultural system into the following eight structures or sub-systems:

1 social structure/social system;
2 economic system;
3 communication system;
4 rationality system;
5 technology system;
6 morality system;
7 belief system;
8 aesthetic system.

A naive Marxist view would be that the technological and economic systems provide the base or substructure which *determine* all other aspects of the cultural system. Several Marxists, for example, Gramsci and Lukacs, as well as neo-Marxists such as Habermas and others of the Frankfurt school, have found this determinism difficult to accept. The assumption behind the following analysis is that all eight sub-systems of the cultural system interact and influence each other. In some cases, such as *communication* and *technology*, or *social* and *economic*, the interaction will be particularly powerful, but the dynamic is always a two-way interaction rather than a simple cause and effect determining relationship.

I will begin by describing and justifying each of the eight systems:

1 Social structure/social system

All societies have some kind of social structure, that is, some system of defining relationships within the society as a whole. Kinship, status, role, duty and obligation are the key social concepts which not only exist in every society, but which have to be passed on to the next generation.

In some societies, social structure is simple and taken for granted; in others, the social system is complex, open to debate and possibly to change. The social structure will be closely related to economic and technological factors; for example, when western European societies were largely rural and agricultural, the dominant factor in social relationship was the possession or non-possession of land; but as trade and industry developed, land became less important than capital, or the ownership of the means of production.

There are various ways of classifying society according to the dominant characteristics of its social structure. Social stratification is an important aspect of most social systems; in capitalist societies social class is very important.

2   Economic system

Every society has some means of dealing with the problem of scarce resources, their distribution and exchange. In some societies, the economic arrangements will be extremely simple, perhaps involving barter; in other societies the economic system will be highly complex. Marxist theory includes an 'evolutionary' sequence from primitive communism to feudalism and capitalism. Varieties of interpretation exist with which to analyse capitalist or post-capitalist social and economic systems. One important measurable feature is the amount of state-ownership existing within societies which are basically capitalist, such as the USA and Western European democracies. Other important measures will include the percentage of a society's wealth and income which are owned by the 'top' 1 per cent, 5 per cent or 10 per cent of the population.

There will also tend to be some direct relation of the economic system to the occupational structure, and therefore to the demand for certain kinds of skills and trained manpower.

When politicians and employers talk of the educational needs of society it is this kind of matching they have in mind. It is my intention, however, not to underestimate the importance of this factor but to put it into a more balanced perspective. Some would say that in a mainly capitalist society it is to be expected that the link between education and economy should be the dominant one. That does not mean that educationists should accept that dominance. One of the purposes of cultural analysis will be to emphasise other features.

3   Communication system

In all societies, human beings communicate with each other. One of the major differences between man and other animals is the existence of human language. Where communication is entirely by means of spoken language most, if not all, of the learning required is informal – even unconscious (children are unaware that they are learning a language, and parents unaware that they are teaching when they provide a speech model).

In many societies, speech is not the only form of communication: American Indians have elaborate sign languages and smoke signals, for example; other societies have developed various kinds of writing; it has often been pointed out by sociologists and social historians that the development of print has made enormous differences to the type of society which developed.[6] Most societies have visual symbols of some importance too. Such non-speech forms of communication are acquired less automatically than speech, and usually some kind of teaching and learning process is involved. When we proceed to the task of distinguishing different societies according to the kinds of communication systems they have, we will need to employ such categories as 'varieties' of spoken language and written language as well as identifying the relative importance of other symbols or signalling systems.

For purposes of educational analysis, the development of writing and of print is of very great significance. This is partly because print potentially makes specialised knowledge more available, but at the same time encourages the tendency for printed 'knowledge' to become highly specialised and therefore less available to the non-specialist reader. In democratic societies with supposedly 'open' systems of education, one of the major curricular problems is, as we shall see, to achieve a balance between general education and specialisation; this is closely connected with the various media available for general and specialised communication.

4 Rationality system

All societies are rational in the sense of having a view about what is 'reasonable' and what counts as an explanation in terms of cause and effect. The particular kinds of explanation may differ, but attempts are always made to explain physical phenomena and human behaviour. Without some kind of rationality any kind of communication would be impossible: words and other signs must be used consistently to make comprehension and co-operation possible – basic rules of meaning and logic are essential. The kind of explanation that is accepted as rational will, however, vary from one society to another or from one time to another within a given society so that whereas one group might explain a man being attracted to a woman in terms of 'love', another group might invoke Freudian theory, another magic or witchcraft. These explanations are seen by anthropologists as different expressions of rationality rather than as being right or wrong explanations.[7]

A useful way of distinguishing and classifying societies may be to categorise them as being 'unified rationality' or 'sub-divided rationality'. Some societies manage to look at the whole of experience through one all-embracing world-view; others, for example Western European cultures, have developed a scientific way of thinking which is different from the religious and different from the poetic, and so on. Levi-Strauss (1966) has also classified societies as 'hot' or 'cold': 'hot' societies are characterised by scientific thinking, whereas 'cold' (primitive) societies are 'time-suppressing' and rely on myth rather than science and history to explain their universe.

5   Technology system

Man everywhere attempts if not to control the environment at least to lessen domination by it. Early man developed tools to build shelter from the climate, and to kill animals for food; later to produce food by various kinds of agriculture. All human beings are 'technologists' in the sense of being tool-users, and make progress by passing on their developing technology, with improvements, to the next generation. Learning to use and to improve tools is always an important feature of cultural life.

In some societies technology is comparatively simple, so differences in access to the technology are almost non-existent. In modern industrial society, on the other hand, no one person could possibly be skilled in all aspects of technology, so specialisation and inequality of access to technological knowledge become problems. In such societies one difficulty is how to cope not only with the transmission of knowledge and skills, but also with the problem of 'allocating' or selecting different individuals for certain kinds of learning: these different learning processes will tend to be given different levels of value or prestige within the social structure. This is the classic division of labour problem described by Marx and Durkheim in their different ways.

It is possible to categorise a society according to the dominant system of technology: is it simple or complex? Is the society at the pre-industrial or post-industrial state of development? It is possible to measure some aspects of technological 'advance' by, for example, quoting the number of cars or television sets per thousand of the population. But no system of educational cultural analysis yet envisaged would require so much detail. Broader categories are quite sufficient. It is perhaps also important to state firmly at this stage in the analysis that no ethnocentric judgment is intended when talking about 'advance' or 'progress' from, for example, pre-industrial to post-industrial. There are advantages and disadvantages in both kinds of society, but the educational requirements will differ to some extent.

6 Morality system

Another characteristic that all human beings have in common is that they possess a sense of 'the moral'; all societies have some kind of code of ethics and distinguish between right and wrong behaviour. What is regarded as right or appropriate varies enormously, but nowhere are there human beings living in a community without a system of morals or ethics. Kluckhohn (1951), for example, suggests that this moral feeling, at least in the form of the existence of a conscience is at least partly biological or genetic. This view would be supported by the studies of Piaget and Kohlberg[8] on the development of moral ideas and ethical behaviour including some cross-cultural studies.

In some societies the moral code is unitary and taken for granted; in other societies, value pluralism exists and the problem of socialising the young is much more difficult – total agreement will be lacking, yet some kind of rules of behaviour need to be transmitted. When moving from cultural invariants to cultural variables the main ways of categorising morality systems would include analysing the dominant system as, for example, religious or secular, and also questioning whether there is a single moral system as in pre-Reformation Europe where the Catholic Church provided a unified moral view, or a variety of competing views as with the moral pluralism in most twentieth century western industrialised societies.

7 Belief system

Closely connected with the morality system is a broader category: the dominant belief system of any society. In some cultures the moral code will be backed up by, and closely related to, religious dogma and perhaps divine revelation or myths about the origins of the community; in other societies these links have become weakened or the prevailing belief system will be entirely secular – for example, having a belief in scientific explanations where 'man is the measure of all things'.

In the latter kind of society, the problem of educating the young and passing on a belief system is much more difficult, not least because the young will be encouraged to question and criticise rather than simply learn and accept.

In classifying societies according to their different kinds of belief system, the following terms would be useful: capitalist, socialist, democratic, totalitarian, liberal, conservative, and so on. There is also some overlap with the categories listed above under 'morality system'. At a deeper level the Kluckhohn/Strodtbeck (1961, page 12) 'Range of Variations' may provide useful insights:

The Five Value Orientations and the Range of
Variations Postulated for Each

Orientation	Postulated Range of Variations					
Human nature	Evil		Neutral	Mixture of good-and-evil	Good	
	mutable	immutable	mutable	immutable	mutable	immutable
Man-nature	Subjugation-to-nature		Harmony-with-nature		Mastery-over-nature	
Time	Past		Present		Future	
Activity	Being		Being-in-becoming		Doing	
Relational	Lineality		Collaterality		Individualism	

Figure 3

8 Aesthetic system

All human beings have aesthetic drives and needs. Every society produces some kind of art and entertainment for its members, even when they are living close to subsistence level. A society's art has standards of form and substance, and is related to the values, technology and social structure of that society. One of the interesting features of human life is the enormous variety of aesthetic forms, but nowhere is a sense of the aesthetic absent.

Raymond Williams (1981) has recently discussed culture in relation to attempts to categorise societies according to aesthetic stages. He analyses and dismisses the view put forward by Lukacs in describing three 'phases' in art: 'the practical, the magico-religious and the aesthetic'. From the point of view of this analysis such evolutionary approaches are not likely to be helpful in the aesthetic field. For our purposes it will be sufficient to take some account of the classification of aesthetic systems in terms of listing and categorising what counts as 'Art' in any society, establishing boundaries between the Arts and examining the relationships between categories. A second useful area of study will include aesthetic morphology – that is, the analysis of form and style in each of the Arts, and the relations between them. Finally, it will be very important to analyse the relation between sub-divisions within the aesthetic system and the other seven systems; in that respect the complex relationship with all the other systems will be particularly important.

Summary of Stage 1: Cultural Invariants

I have attempted to analyse in brief outline those characteristics that all human societies appear to have in common. Any human group which did not possess all of those eight features would not qualify for the title of 'society'. To some extent, the eight characteristics are derived from conventional, sociological or anthropological definitions of society but, to some extent, they are empirical – no anthropologist has ever found a group of human beings living permanently together that lacked any one of these eight characteristics.

In addition to suggesting that all cultures must possess the eight systems, I also hypothesise that all societies have means of transmitting these systems from one generation to the next. Some societies will achieve this cultural transmission partly by educational institutions, including formal schooling. Where 'education' of this kind exists certain features must, by definition, always be present. For example, education must involve 'improvement' of some kind, although societies may differ about what constitutes improvement. Such differences are not random, however, and they can easily be exaggerated; it is helpful to begin by looking for invariants rather than variables. (See Peters (1966) for the link between ethics and education.)

I also argue that a satisfactory educational programme must pass on the essentials of the eight systems, unless there are other agencies within society better equipped for that aspect of cultural transmission.

The argument is deliberately circular: if curriculum is defined as a selection from culture, then care must be taken to ensure that the selection is an adequate one; culture can be sub-divided into eight systems, so an adequate selection must include all eight – unless we can be assured that transmission takes place outside education.

NOTES

1   It would, unfortunately, be misleading to suggest that all anthropologists are agreed on these definitions. Keesing (1971) points out that Goodenough (1961) has argued that a distinction *should* be made between patterns *for* behaviour and patterns *of* behaviour: 'culture' has been used to refer to two quite different orders. First, 'culture' has been used to refer to the pattern of life within a community – the observable phenomena; second, 'culture' has been restricted to the organised system of knowledge and belief whereby a people structure their experience – emphasising ideas rather than things. Goodenough and Keesing see advantages in the narrower definition.

2   This Geertz definition is clearly close to the Goodenough-Keesing position referred to in Note 1 above.

3   Why should conservatism among teachers be regarded as 'natural'? One of the reasons for the existence of schools is to transmit 'what is known'; if the rate of change is rapid then schools are inevitably behind the times to some extent. There is also a tendency for teachers to teach *what* they were taught in the *way* they were taught. To avoid this danger, *conscious* efforts have to be made. On the other hand, it can be argued that real education is necessarily subversive – because it teaches the young what might be as well as what is!

4 Jean Floud (1962) and others have argued that an important role for teachers to play is to act in a counter-cyclical direction, to avoid the trendy or the fashionable and to insist on standards which may be enshrined in their own disciplines.

5 Paul Hirst (1975) in the UK has argued in terms of seven forms of knowledge; Philip Phenix (1964) has put forward a view of curriculum based on 'realms of meaning'. Both have been criticised for adopting a cognitive, philosophical position which ignores or underplays the sociological.

6 See, for example, the paper by Goody and Watt in Musgrave (ed.), (1970), page 79.

> In non-literate society every social situation cannot but bring the individual into contact with the group patterns of thought, feeling and action . . . In a literate society however . . . the mere fact that reading and writing are solitary activities means that in so far as the dominant cultural tradition is a literate one, it is very easy to avoid . . .

The importance of this view and its relation to the alienation of the young in urban, industrial societies, seems to me to have been neglected.

7 Anthropologists are not unanimous, however, in their views on cultural beliefs such as magic or witchcraft. Some would regard magic as prescientific (like alchemy), others as a straight alternative to scientific reasoning; others would declare a limit to cultural relativism and declare witchcraft to be a kind of cultural dead-end not capable of justification within the conventional meaning of 'rational'.

8 Kohlberg has been responsible for refining and elaborating on Piaget's notion of moral development in very important ways. Kohlberg has found that the same kind of moral development takes place in a variety of cultures: the sequence of development appears to be invariable although there are some differences in the average age at which the six stages are attained. See Kohlberg (1964) or Lawton (1981) for a summary.

4 Cultural Analysis as Applied to One Society: England

> In most societies for most of recorded time, education has been a reactionary force rather than a progressive one.
>
> Adam Curle*

In chapter 3, I identified eight systems as the most significant cultural invariants for purposes of educational planning. The next stage is to look at one society across those eight parameters not only as a basis for making comparisons, but also as a way of describing and analysing a given society which will then make it possible to plan an educational programme or to improve the curriculum for that society.

Stage 2: Cultural Variables

So we pass from a study of the essential similarities between all human societies (cultural invariants) to a consideration of societal differences or cultural variables (Stage 2 on figure 1 in chapter 3). No two societies are the same in all respects, and it might be expected that educational systems would accordingly differ. One of the interesting features of schools, however, is that they resemble each other so much in all parts of the world. Classrooms in many different countries are almost indistinguishable from each other despite the social and cultural differences which exist. One reason for this is that school structures and education practices tend to be copied from other countries which are supposedly more 'developed'; another reason is the tendency for schools to suffer from 'culture lag' and 'curriculum inertia' – they fail to keep up

---

* (1964) 'Education, Politics and Development', *Comparative Education Review*.

with the social change of their own societies. So the typical school programme is one which was adopted second-hand (rather than thought out from first principles) and which has failed to make appropriate adjustments as society has changed. And it may not have been very good in the first place!

At this stage it is necessary to move, temporarily, away from generalisations about all societies and to choose some descriptive examples from one society. I have taken the easy way out and chosen to analyse the society I know best – England. Perhaps because I am not English,[1] it may be possible for me to retain that certain degree of objectivity which anthropologists recommend.

I will use the eight systems discussed in chapter 3 as headings for a cultural analysis of modern England. When I first embarked upon this exercise, I half expected that someone must already have covered this ground: there are so many sociological studies of the social structure of modern Britain, that it seemed reasonable to assume that a cultural analysis of some kind had been attempted which would have covered most, if not all, of the eight parameters. This appears not to be the case. From the various texts examined, it proved to be impossible to find a 'ready-made cultural analysis'. I will therefore work through these eight headings, in each case giving further references for those who wish to go further into any one or more of the parameters. In some cases the description and analysis will be much more straightforward than in others.

At this stage I want to introduce another very important feature of the analysis. During the course of this analysis, some important *cultural contradictions* will be detected. These contradictions are important not only for social reasons, but for their educational and curricular implications. For example, the idea of equality of opportunity is contradicted by the existence and defence of such privileges as the 'right' to buy access to certain kinds of education-al institutions – for example, independent schools. The existence of cultural contradictions has a long history, but has not received adequate attention from the socio-educational point of view. In different ways Marx and Weber have referred to contradictions in various parts of the world as part of a general analysis. Tawney and others have referred, for example, to social justice and class in England. Some writers have preferred to talk in terms of hypoc-risy; others, such as Edmund King (1979) have referred to paradoxes. These are features of all societies, but several writers have drawn particular attention to cultural contradictions within English society.[2]

1   Social system

Many volumes have been written about English social structure. Only a few major subheadings can be suggested here, and I will avoid going into statistical detail.

In terms of Cattell's most important classification, size, it is necessary to note that England is a large society numerically and has a sizeable population compared with the land available. It is one of the most densely populated areas in the world. It is an urban industrial society with growing problems of social control: crime, juvenile delinquency, vandalism – and general unrest among the young – are all on the increase.

It would appear that the general problem of how to cope with young people growing up in an industrial society – especially in inner city, over-crowded areas – has been seriously underestimated by politicians, administrators and educationists. When there is added to these problems the additional difficulties of accommodating immigrant minorities,[3] a series of crises develop – social, political and educational as well as economic.

An important factor which complicates and aggravates the problem of urban, industrial society is class. The complexity of the English class system is baffling to outsiders (including some sociologists). Class also influences and sometimes dominates other aspects of social life – perhaps every aspect of English social life, including education and industry (the 'old boy' network is more powerful in England than, say, in Japan, Germany or the USA).

Despite the fact that the class structure retains noticeable feudal vestiges (the House of Lords, the Monarchy, a system of titles, and so on), England claims to be a democratic and open society. This is one of the cultural contradictions referred to above. Ideals such as 'equal opportunity' are enshrined in social and educational legislation, but as sociologists have demonstrated *ad nauseam*, the ideal is very far from the reality.

2   Economic system

England has to be classified as a highly industrialised society which is experiencing great difficulties in retaining its place among the most developed and prosperous industrialised countries. It relies heavily on its ability to export manufactured goods in order to pay for 'essential' imports including food: only about one-third of food is home-grown, and it is doubtful whether the country could support its large population by growing more food, even with dramatic changes in diet.[4]

Not only is England a highly industrialised society, it was the first country to undergo the 'Industrial Revolution'. This gave England considerable economic advantages in the eighteenth and nineteenth centuries which have become disadvantages in the twentieth: other countries have learned the lessons of industrialisation in its later phases more easily than England which is, to some extent, handicapped by its 'pre-industrial' social structure and attitudes. In addition, England has had to face the difficulties of ceasing to be an imperial power with captive overseas markets and easy sources of cheap raw materials.

In brief, the dominant economic feature of British society is that it no longer finds it easy to 'earn its living'; imports exceed exports in most years; unemployment is high, despite the shortage of some skilled labour; the real standard of living is in decline.

At a time of economic decline, social and educational contradictions are likely to loom larger – probably including a widening gap between rich and poor in terms of welfare and educational provision.

Another feature of English society is that its economic system is still basically a capitalist one which has succeeded in withstanding many of the advances of welfare state socialism. The British version of a mixed economy and multinational capitalism is unique, and allows a good deal of wealth and power to remain within the control of 'the ruling class'.

3 Communication system

It is now possible, as a result of various linguistic surveys, not only to state with some accuracy how many people in England speak English as their native language, but also to locate the vast number of minority languages which are spoken as first or second languages.[5]

It is equally possible to make reasonably accurate statements about varieties of English such as dialects and the specialised registers within the English language.

English is clearly the dominant speech form, but to say that is not helpful in educational planning; it is merely to state the obvious. The English also have a reputation for failing to respect the language customs of linguistic minorities: at various times in British history the languages of the Welsh, the Scots and the Irish have been deliberately suppressed or forbidden. More recently, the difficulties of immigrants speaking another language (for example, those from the Indian subcontinent) or speaking a non-standard dialect (those from the West Indies) have not been given sufficient resources or even sympathy. Similarly, until relatively recently the existence of non-standard forms of working-class language was seen only as a problem, and dialects were generally regarded as deviant forms needing to be eradicated.

But English is not the only form of communication. A scientific, industrialised society uses mathematics to communicate; in a democratic society, much vital information is communicated by statistical symbols, charts and diagrams; increasingly it is suggested that we need to learn computer languages; many signs and symbols have to be used or at least understood in order to facilitate survival in an urban, industrialised society, for example, complex systems of road signs.

The division of labour produced by industrialisation, combined with the development of printing, also poses problems of communication within a democratic society. There are specialised vocabularies and other linguistic features which those not inducted into the specialism find difficult to comprehend.

The existence of the mass media in a society like England is also an important feature of the communication system which cannot be ignored by educational institutions. Richard Hoggart (1960) in *Uses of Literacy* pointed out the opportunities presented by the popular press as well as the problems associated with them, and the failure of the educational system so far to cope with that problem. More recently, other studies have indicated both the need for education to cope with radio and television, and some of the problems inherent in the existence of these media.

4   Rationality system

In the terminology used by Claude Levi-Strauss, England is a 'hot' culture. It copes with rapid social and technological change by a system of rationality which can 'explain' change, and regards change as normal. In England this kind of scientific rationality is associated historically with the Protestant Reformation of the sixteenth and seventeenth centuries which questioned authority and led to 'rational' explanation of the universe. Newtonian science sought to provide a rule system which would explain the physical universe; the *laissez-faire* economics of Adam Smith, and the utilitarian philosophy of Bentham and Mill, attempted to find the equivalent of Newtonian scientific method to apply to human behaviour.

I suggested above that it might be useful to classify societies into those which are governed by a unified 'rationality' and those where rationality is subdivided into various 'forms of knowledge'. In England one of the forms of knowledge – the 'scientific' kind – appears to be dominant. The high status of science has not only distorted the disciplines involved in the study of human behaviour – hence discussions of 'positivism' in the social sciences – it has also obscured the need to understand other ways of thinking and evaluating what might be applied to the aesthetic and other experiences. As we shall see in a later section, this has direct relevance to education where 'utilitarian' thinking has tended to become dominant.

5 Technology system

In a modern industrial society, technology is enormously complex. So much so that no one individual can be expected to master the whole of technology, just as no one individual knows the meaning of all the words in a modern dictionary.

Specialisation is inevitable, but a distinction needs to be made between doing and understanding: it may not be either possible or desirable for the whole population to have the skills necessary to work as a physicist in a nuclear power station, but it is desirable for the majority to have sufficient knowledge to be able to understand the kinds of dangers involved in that kind of technology and to be able to assess the risks involved for the whole community. A problem of differential access to knowledge already existed before the advent of microtechnology and the so-called computer revolution. But with these developments, society may be dangerously divided into those who can master information retrieval (those who know how to find out), and those who have not acquired such mastery. This is, of course, a problem which Britain shares with the rest of the highly industrialised world, but it may have particular difficulties in England because of the class structure and certain peculiarities of educational institutions which will be discussed later.

The relationship between education and work (and therefore technology) is an extremely important one to resolve. In England, the debate is sometimes about whether schools should be concerned with vocational training or not. In reality, the problem is much more complex than that.

At least two points need to be made at this stage of our analysis. The first concerns the paradox (or cultural contradiction) that despite the fact that England was first into the field of industrialisation on a large scale, it has never been socially acceptable to be an industrialist or to work in industry. Industry and commerce were seen throughout the nineteenth century, and well into the twentieth century, as inferior occupations incompatible with the status of being a gentleman. The disastrous consequences of this 'feudal vestige' have been pointed out by Weiner (1981), Roderick and Stevens (1981) and many others.

A separate but related point has been made by Raymond Williams. He has pointed out that since the seventeenth century science and technology have been seen as separate developments and not integrated into the major thought systems of English society. This has not only produced the kind of two cultures society (science and arts) described by C. P. Snow,[6] but it has also impoverished the humanities. Both of these attitudes, contradictions or failures, are connected with the idea that work of a practical nature, including technology and applied science, is not suitable for a gentleman,[7] and therefore should be kept out of 'real' education.

Another interesting cultural contradiction related to technology is that although England was the first country to become highly industrialised, the process of socialising the workers into accepting the work ethic has never been totally successful. The contrast between the attitudes of British workers and those in, say, Hong Kong, Singapore, Japan, or even Western Germany, is not just the propaganda of middle-class oriented newspapers. Edward Thompson (1968) has lucidly described the difficulties of disciplining the workers in the eighteenth and nineteenth centuries, and the damage caused to their cultural life, but the process was never complete. In many respects, England is more a 'play culture' than a work culture: it is surely no coincidence that the English have invented and developed so many sports and games. Other aspects of the play culture would include: the amount of time devoted to leisure pursuits in newspapers and on television programmes; the popularity of holiday programmes on radio and television; even the fact that English crossword puzzles are allegedly more difficult (and therefore more time-consuming) than anywhere else – all these are indications of a deep-rooted cultural characteristic.[8]

In the recent past, these national characteristics have been seen as great handicaps in a fiercely competitive international trade climate, but at a time when work may be coming of less importance in our culture, then it may turn out to be an advantage in some respects.

6   Morality system

England is now an example of 'moral pluralism', in which a largely secular morality is dominant. It would be difficult to regard England as a Christian society in any meaningful sense, despite the continued existence of the established Church and the assumption often made that 'religion' means the Christian religion. Since the Reformation and the seventeenth century Puritan revolution, the idea of a single uncontroversial moral system has been progressively weakened. Not only did the State church (the Church of England) split up into a number of denominations, sects and heresies, but also the whole notion of religious and moral *authority* was increasingly questioned. Newtonian science challenged one accepted view of the world, and this investigatory attitude later spread from the physical universe to studies of the nature of man himself. By the late nineteenth century a mixture of utilitarianism and Christian principles provided the main basis for moral thinking, but the two sources were often in opposition and provided yet another example of a cultural contradiction within English society.[9] In the twentieth century, especially after World War II, immigration from non-Christian societies further complicated the moral scene. Another difficulty which has gradually emerged is the fact that law and morality are increasingly seen as separate issues. One danger in that situation is an aspect of what Durkheim referred to as 'anomie' – not knowing what the rules of society really are; a second, and connected, danger is the retreat to moral relativism – the suggestion that morality is simply a matter of taste, or that one rule or rule system is as good as any other.

7   Belief system

In one respect, the problems of the belief system and the related value systems are similar to the difficulties of the moral system discussed above; there appears to be no consensus, and there is the complicating danger of relativism and anomie. But the belief system is even more complex.

In terms of the Kluckhohn and Strodtbeck model discussed in chapter 3, the English value system might be classified for each of five orientations as follows:

(a) **Human nature** is a mixture of good and evil; it is mutable: much tends to be made of the influence of the environment over human development, so much so that there is sometimes a danger of exaggerating the 'determining' influence of environment and consequently neglecting free will.

(b) **Man-nature**. The English assume that they have mastery over nature. Technology is seen as a means of mastery and it is assumed that almost everything is possible.

(c) **Time**. This is difficult because although it would seem that the dominant orientation is the future, it is also true that much lip-service is paid to respect for tradition. Another cultural contradiction?

(d) **Activity**. Doing appears much more important than being – English pragmatism may well be connected with this.

(e) **Relational**. The dominant orientation would seem to be individualism, hence related problems of developing a *socially* acceptable moral code.

Such a classification may serve as a useful background to a cultural analysis, but – as we shall see in the next chapter – choices still have to be made. It would not be appropriate to say, for instance, that because the English are individualist that education should encourage this trait. Perhaps schools should aim at a more balanced personality by countering individualism by training for co-operation.

More specifically, it would be important to classify England as a democratic society – or at least one which claims to be democratic. It is also a society where capitalism is moderated to some extent by a welfare state; there is some suspicion of the values of capitalism including acquisitiveness and uncontrolled selfish individualism. More contradictions!

8   Aesthetic system

In terms of Raymond Williams' (1980) discussion of Lukacs, English society has moved out of the magico-religious phase into the aesthetic phase (with some vestigial remains): some kinds of 'work' which meet no practical need are valued, but are not taken to be evidence of some metaphysical or superhuman dimension of reality. Art has been almost completely secularised, but in the process has been – often quite artificially – separated from everyday life. A number of problems emerge for a society at this stage, especially where the value system is pluralistic rather than unified. What counts as art is one problem; even more difficult is what counts as good art. At a time of rapid social and technological change the rules or criteria of excellence are blurred or even completely open to public debate.

Problems of the aesthetic system are related to problems and contradictions within the social structure. What is classified as art and subject to aesthetic criteria tend to be what I discussed earlier as the artefacts of high culture associated with the upper and upper middle classes, whereas other phenomena which should be susceptible to aesthetic criteria appear to be treated differently – not least in education. The art correspondents of 'serious' newspapers rarely, if ever, discuss the aesthetic qualities of motor cars or hi-fi sets; the art and architecture criteria which apply to public buildings are not considered appropriate to the interior decorating of 'ordinary' homes; gardening, which might plausibly be described as the most pervasive art form in England, is not taken seriously by aesthetic experts except for the elite landscaped gardens of stately homes. The assumption is always that different rules apply or that more modest everyday phenomena are not worthy of serious aesthetic consideration. The false divorce of high culture from popular culture, combined with much confusion about the 'tests of truth' procedures, has created a highly dangerous social situation and one which poses enormous problems for education. Some very interesting insights are contained in Nikolaus Pevsner's book *The Englishness of English Art*.

In chapter 5 an attempt will be made to look at the existing curricula in England and to match them against the kind of cultural analysis outlined in this chapter. From that analysis will emerge possible changes and reforms in school curricula.

Summary

The cultural analysis sketched in this chapter demonstrates the existence of a number of difficulties and problems, some of them associated with basic contradictions within English society. All societies have contradictions which give rise to productive tension; but some advanced industrial societies may be so racked with serious contradictions as to be in danger of breakdown. This was precisely Durkheim's fear: post-Reformation and post-revolutionary France left a society without a clear belief system or moral code.

One of the most disturbing results of a cultural analysis of this kind is that it seems to indicate a society which is not only in decline economically, but has reached crisis point in a number of other systems – social and moral as well as in the basic belief system. One danger is that education will be blamed for the crises; another is that too much will be expected of education in a society which may be unwilling to face the task of resolving its deep-rooted cultural contradictions.

NOTES

1 I hesitate to introduce autobiography into a book of this kind, but it may be of significance to note that since I come from the Celtic fringe, being half-Welsh and half-Irish, it may be that I can see English society more as an outsider and thus preserve a certain detachment. Partly for that reason, I have deliberately chosen to discuss 'England' rather than 'England and Wales' or 'the UK'.

2 Tawney's book *Equality* (1931) is still a classic in the field; Professor Edmund King's cross-cultural studies of education are also relevant especially since he has made much of the importance of the 'gentleman ideal' in English education. See in particular his *Other Schools and Ours* (1979).

3 It should perhaps be made clear that there is no reason why immigration as such *should* be a problem; ideally we would be able to regard the children of immigrants as enriching the native culture. Immigration does, however, become a problem – social rather than educational, when already inadequate resources such as housing appear to become even more inadequate.

4 There is some argument about this. It probably depends on *how* dramatic a change in diet would be regarded as politically acceptable – much less meat presumably, which would be seen as a substantial lowering of the standard of living.

5 The Linguistic Minorities Project (LMP) directed by Dr Verity Khan, at the University of London Institute of Education is involved in this work, producing data for the Department of Education and Science (DES).

6   C. P. Snow (1905–80), Lord Snow of Leicester. A scientist and novelist as well as a politician, Snow read a paper on 'The Two Cultures and the Scientific Revolution', the 1959 Rede Lecture at Cambridge, in which he criticised the educational system for producing scientists and arts graduates who could not communicate with each other: scientists who failed to read and 'humanists' who could not understand the second law of thermodynamics. The lecture caused a good deal of discussion and has been much quoted ever since, but it was no more than a revival of the nineteenth-century debate between scientists and humanists.

7   Frank Musgrove's work (1979) suggests that the dominant culture in England is not bourgeois but 'gentry' – not books but bloodsports! Edmund King has also written extensively on this topic from the point of view of Comparative Education, and Michael Young raised some important issues in his satirical work *The Rise of the Meritocracy* (1958).

8   There are at least two different ways of interpreting this evidence about sport: it could illustrate a healthy attitude to recreation; or it might be evidence of another kind of 'opium for the masses'!

9   R. H. Tawney's *Religion and the Rise of Capitalism* (1926) is an excellent study which shows, *inter alia*, the incompatibility of capitalism and traditional Christianity. The nineteenth century and early twentieth century 'Christian Socialist' movement could be seen as a revival of anti-capitalist Christian ethics reacting against *laissez-faire* economics and utilitarian social policies.

5 A Selection from the Culture

The question, then, is how to reduce over-adjustment, conformity and anomie, and how to support individuality, creativity and autonomy in the mass age?

Hilda Taba*

Education has an important part to play in advanced industrial societies, as Durkheim clearly saw. Whereas in simple societies a socialisation process emerges more or less automatically out of the eight cultural systems, in a complex and contradictory society such as England, education needs very careful planning if it is to help society to survive. But in England, as in some other societies, traditional patterns of education and schooling have continued long after they have ceased to provide adequate service for young people. A common temptation is to make minor adjustments to the traditional educational structure and curriculum when what is required is a complete rethinking of education from basic principles.

Radical plans must, however, always be interpreted realistically – that is, in terms of 'piecemeal social engineering' rather than a Utopian master plan. One of the lessons learned from a wide range of educational research is that any reform must *start* (but not finish) from where teachers are now. Part of the following planning procedure will, therefore, be concerned with comparing the 'needs' thrown up by the cultural analysis with what the existing teachers can provide. Even with massive retraining programmes it would still be necessary to start from the current position of the teaching profession. I want to begin this part of the curriculum plan by assuming, on the basis of an ample amount of evidence,[1] that the teaching profession is a reasonably competent group of

* (1962) *Curriculum Development.*

individuals doing a difficult job sometimes under almost impossible conditions. There is no reason to believe that as a profession they are any less efficient, hardworking or caring than doctors or solicitors, for example. A major problem at the moment is that society does not really know what to expect of them.

One of the most frequently advanced arguments about schools is that they should present to their pupils a 'balanced curriculum'. The debate in England about the curriculum since 1976 included much reference to the desirability of 'balance' – a view which has been taken severely to task by Robert Dearden (1981). The balanced curriculum metaphor is an interesting one. Presumably either 'balance' is regarded as a good quality in its own right, or the idea of a balanced curriculum rests upon an analogy with the idea of a balanced diet. This may be a useful analogy up to a point, but it should be used very carefully. One of the problems is that the idea of a balanced diet rests on reasonably well established scientific data in the field of nutrition about vitamins, proteins, carbohydrates, minerals, and so on. There is general agreement about the components of a balanced diet; but there is no such agreement about the 'ingredients' in a balanced curriculum. As Dearden points out, discussion of a balanced curriculum is meaningless unless there is some kind of prior commitment to curricular 'ingredients'. This is precisely what is lacking in most discussions of a balanced curriculum, including recent official statements such as *The School Curriculum* (1981).

I want to proceed to the next part of the curriculum planning process by saying that a balanced curriculum will be one which does not neglect any one of the eight systems discussed in the previous chapters. In Dearden's terms, I have a prior commitment to each of those eight aspects of culture. I can, legitimately, describe a balanced curriculum on the basis of those eight systems. They are all indispensable; so let us assume that they are all equally important unless it can be otherwise demonstrated. This is a principle which might in itself do something to redress the balance in favour of neglected areas of the curriculum such as the political, the moral and the aesthetic. Essentially the task of improving the curriculum will be to identify gaps in the existing school programmes from the cultural analysis I have already outlined. In addition to gaps there will be 'mismatches', that is, content which is out of date or otherwise inappropriate.

In this part of the planning, the first question would therefore be to see to what extent the eight systems are covered by existing school subjects; the second would be to evaluate the quality or appropriateness of the coverage where it exists at all. To avoid unnecessary repetition, I will deal with both of these issues at the same time, going through the eight systems one by one. It will also be important to see to what extent any 'system' is, or could be, catered for by agencies outside formal education.

1   Social system

England is a complex, urban society, with a very complicated political and social structure. But most young people leave school almost entirely ignorant of that structure. This has been demonstrated by a number of surveys of young school leavers, notably by publications of the Hansard Society.[2]

England is an industrialised society, but education has failed to enable the young to live harmoniously within that society: they have a very imperfect understanding of industrialisation; many of them are not educated in such a way as to gain employment, or to be able to cope with unemployment by being educated for leisure.

England is a democratic society with a high rate of social mobility. But schools still tend to divide the young socially, academically and culturally, rather than to encourage co-operation, social harmony and the development of a common culture.

These are a few of the cultural contradictions connected with the social structure. Clearly, they also overlap with some of the other seven systems.

Part of the gap-filling exercise would be to propose that no secondary school curriculum should be regarded as adequate unless it contained a reasonable amount of time devoted to the social sciences including a suitable programme of political literacy. This was, in effect, one of the recommendations of Her Majesty's Inspectorate (HMI) document *Curriculum 11–16* (1977); some of Her Majesty's Inspectors (HMIs) also showed concern about this 'gap' when they recommended that this aspect of culture should be included in the APU[3] national testing programme, but that part of the programme has been abandoned. Filling this gap need not involve a new subject on the timetable (see Crick and Porter, 1979): what is needed is an acceptance by teachers (as well as LEAs and governors) that the social and political aspects of our culture represent a very important kind of knowledge and experience which should be dealt with by the school.

Apart from the problem of schools where the gap exists, there is also the problem of 'mismatch': schools who cope with 'the problem' by Mickey Mouse Social Studies – 'how a Bill becomes an Act', but not a word about 'interest groups' or the distribution of power in society.

2 Economic system

There are two major educational implications emerging from the analysis of the economic system in chapter 4. The first relates to the need for the young to understand the economic system; the second is the much more frequently discussed assertion that the curriculum should enable the young to take part in that part of the economic system euphemistically referred to as 'the world of work'.

The first is easy to accept but may be difficult to accommodate within existing curricular structures. Most young people leave school with very little understanding of the economic system. Economics is taught in many schools (especially to boys) but it tends to be an *option* for the 14+ age-group rather than part of the common curriculum. The remedy is obvious; let it become part of a common programme for all pupils (girls and boys) preferably starting at an earlier age – some useful work can be included in the primary curriculum.[4]

If economics is to become part of the common curriculum within an integrated social science or humanities programme, then the content will have to be looked at carefully. Existing GCE 'O' level syllabuses tend to be far too abstract and distanced from everyday concerns. Not all CSE syllabuses succeed in avoiding this trap, but some do and they could serve as useful models for a common programme. This is not to suggest that abstract concepts should be avoided, merely that they should be suitably grounded in the meaningful. All young people should leave school with an understanding of such concepts as *supply and demand*, the *market*, *exports* and *imports*, *balance of payments* and so on, as well as the ability to make sense of elementary statistics presented in a variety of forms.

The second implication was that schools should prepare the young for the economic system. This is more controversial. If it means that the curriculum should go some way towards helping the young to earn a living, then there can be little objection to this statement. If, however, it is suggested that an important function of the school is to supply industry with suitable manpower, the ideological difficulties begin to emerge. Those who object to the present economic system for its exploitation of workers can hardly be expected to socialise the young to accept exploitation by developing acceptable habits of obedience and subservience.

However, a distinction needs to be made between the general education of the young which would include developing attitudes and skills which would help in earning a living in a variety of occupations, and narrow vocational training (including attitudes) which would slot school leavers into specific jobs.

There is also a difference between sensibly adjusting the school curriculum to match economic and industrial changes (for example, by developing computer studies or microtechnology) and allowing the curriculum to be dominated by the supposed 'needs of industry'.

3   Communication system

English language is certainly taken seriously as a school subject in English schools, but it is taught in a very limited way from the point of view of communication. Official reports dating from the 1920s to the more recent Bullock Report (1975) have diagnosed various shortcomings in the teaching of English as a mother tongue. Two points need to be stressed: first, the neglect of oral language or 'oracy'; second, the failure of most schools to develop a policy of language across the curriculum, that is, to treat English as more than a school subject and to regard the teaching of that form of communication as the responsibility of all teachers. The failure to develop a policy of language across the curriculum is also connected with a failure to get to grips with various specialist forms of language – linguistic varieties such as the language of science – and also a failure to relate 'everyday' language to the academic language of the classroom.[5]

But English is not the only form of communication. A scientific industrialised society uses mathematical symbols to communicate; much vital information is also communicated by statistical symbols, charts and diagrams; increasingly it is suggested that we all need to learn computer languages or at least a sufficient understanding of computer systems to type in our requirements and make use of retrieval systems; many signs and symbols also have to be used or at least understood for survival in an urban, industrial society. Most schools do comparatively little to equip the young adequately for communication in the kind of society which has been described.

Adequate education and communication would also include film studies and television studies including studies of advertising techniques. This kind of reform, including the introduction of 'communication studies', need not involve new subjects on the timetable nor a new breed of teachers. (See chapter 6.)

3   The rationality system

The kind of reasoning or 'view of the world' which tends to dominate English culture is associated with the kind of thinking processes which have developed in the physical sciences since the seventeenth century. This kind of reasoning certainly needs to be covered adequately within the curriculum, but two points need to be made: first, many children 'learn' science without really understanding the basic scientific method of reasoning; second, they are not taught to distinguish between scientific reasoning and other 'forms of knowledge' – for example, the different ways of thinking and feeling required in appreciating poetry, music or art.[6] This is related to the point made in earlier chapters that English society, in common with other Western industrialised societies, has a system of rationality which is not unified but has tended to become subdivided; so we make distinctions between a religious experience and an aesthetic experience, for example, which is completely absent in some other societies. These differences have to be taught and it is a function of the curriculum to plan the learning processes required. It is not suggested that we appoint teachers of rationality – merely that curriculum planning must take account of the complexities of this system by finding ways of identifying opportunities for highlighting issues within a reformed curriculum structure. The Schools Council Science Project directed by Dick West promises to cover some of this field.

5   Technology system

In England, as in many other advanced industrial societies, technology is enormously complex. No one individual can be expected to master the whole of the technology system. Specialisation is inevitable, but schools have a responsibility not simply to train specialists, but to enable all young people to have a general understanding of technology and its place in modern Britain.

The educational problem is two-fold: it is partly a question of curriculum and partly a question of the status of the subject. Even in those schools where a subject such as Craft, Design and Technology (CDT) or Design Technology is on offer, it is almost without exception an option for the 14+ age-group rather than part of the common curriculum. It also tends to be regarded as a subject suitable for the less able rather than for the academically gifted. A reformed curriculum would need to include both kinds of change: that is, technology as part of the common curriculum 14–16 (for girls and boys) and with suitable encouragement being given for all pupils to continue with the study after 16. Careful attention will be needed in constructing both the common curriculum and the specialised courses for the post-16 age-groups of various ability levels. Many excellent ideas contained in the Schools Council *Project Technology* failed to make a real impact on schools because it was regarded as a low status (however interesting) non-examination subject.

In many schools it will be necessary, therefore, to make technology a subject for all pupils on the timetable; in others it may be possible to incorporate technology with science (which up to 16 will be integrated science rather than physics, chemistry and biology). If this route is taken, and it is not undesirable in principle, then great care should be taken to ensure that more than lip service is paid to technology. (See HMI *Technology in Schools* (1982) for detailed suggestions in this field.)

Apart from technology as a subject, it will also be necessary to ensure that adequate attention is paid to technology by other subject teachers – for example, in history and geography. History teachers, for example, are often very good at making the Industrial Revolution exciting, but neglect to show the historical and social importance of technological developments in the nineteenth and twentieth centuries.

The most important educational goal is to encourage teachers and pupils to recognise that technology is a vitally important feature of our culture, and one which is worthy of the best minds.

It will also be important to relate the technology system to other systems especially the aesthetic. Sir Alex Smith, when he was Chairman of the Schools Council, often suggested that children of all ages should be required, as part of every year's curriculum, to design and make a suitable object. Aesthetic criteria as well as the functional would be involved in the evaluation of such exercises.

6 The morality system

This is arguably the most serious gap in the curriculum in English schools. England can no longer be regarded as a Christian society; values are increasingly secular; society is multicultural and plural in other respects; yet schools are required to persist with compulsory religious instruction (usually of a vaguely Christian kind) and a compulsory daily act of worship. This is perhaps the clearest example of curriculum inertia and cultural lag. Little attempt has been made to teach elementary ethics as Dearden (1968) recommended. Few schools take the idea of moral autonomy seriously.[7]

Some schools and LEAs have made much more progress than others. At least one LEA has encouraged the use of 'tutor group time'[8] for discussion of practical moral questions along the lines advocated by Leslie Button (1981–2). Others use, for example, Peter McPhail's *Lifeline* materials.

There is no one best solution, but certain principles can be asserted: the first is that some *time* must be made available, not necessarily for a new subject but for teachers and pupils to look specifically at ethical and moral issues. As we shall see in chapter 6, a school policy as a preliminary structure should precede the drawing up of detailed syllabuses.

In addition, it will be necessary at school level to discuss what contributions other subjects such as English and history have to make to pupils' moral development. It should not be left to chance. And teachers will probably need some training in this difficult area before embarking on controversial issues. It has also been suggested (see Richard Pring, 1982) that for schools to encourage moral development in a satisfactory way, they will need to become better examples of moral institutions – in other words, practice what they preach.

7 The belief system

Reference has already been made to the fact that a basic element of the belief system is that England is a democratic society, or a society attempting to be democratic. The basic contradiction here is that not only do public schools and various other forms of independent schools exist, but even within the state system equality of opportunity is very far from being a reality. A major need is for a properly planned common curriculum which will give access to the major kinds of educational knowledge and experiences to all young people.

There are other examples of difficulties of contradictions within the belief system which are less easy to identify. The major problem is that there is no longer a single value or belief system which can be accepted in its entirety; English society is characterised by value pluralism. It is, however, still necessary for schools to work out what beliefs and values are held in common or need to be held in common, and therefore should be transmitted by means of the school curriculum. Here we are back to the situation described by Durkheim: without some kind of common value system, society will be in danger of collapse. It is no use suggesting that transmission of values can be left to families: it is precisely because there are differences within the society between families and other social groups that there needs to be a common system of beliefs worked out which can be transmitted on a consensus basis via the school curriculum. This is a clear example of a kind of knowledge or value system which if not transmitted by the school will not be transmitted at all.

Teachers in England sometimes sneer at such American practices as 'saluting the flag', but schools in the USA have been used quite successfully to inculcate immigrants with the idea of 'the nation'. Schools in England have, in fact, been preaching patriotism in a variety of ways, only marginally more subtle than the American practices – for example, by 'suitable' history and geography textbooks. In recent years, however, the virtues of patriotism have been called into question, and schools are now more likely to wish to promote 'international understanding' or 'multiculturalism'. These are much more difficult, but if this is what we want schools to aim at, then we must be much clearer about the means.

There are some ideas and concepts which can be 'understood' at the cognitive level – for example, 'democracy' – without giving young people an appropriate experience really to appreciate that quality. The difficulty with some aspects of a belief system is that they can only be fully appreciated if experienced in some meaningful way. This would argue for students in schools having some kind of democratic practice or experience as part of school life. This is not to suggest that schools should become democracies (electing head teachers, and so on), but that schools should be somewhat more democratic and should involve democratic experiences of some kind for all pupils.

Similar arguments might be employed regarding other desirable attitudes such as tolerance. It is easy to bring about some understanding of what is roughly meant by tolerance, but it is much more difficult to change a young person in the direction of tolerance. In this respect it has to be said many schools are extremely intolerant of views and tastes which are different from those of the ruling hierarchy (or in some cases, the head). Hair styles and clothing are often condemned for reasons no better than personal taste. Hardly good training in either democracy or tolerance!

Needless to say, it is also easier to teach the idea of tolerance than the reasonable limits of toleration: at what point in a democratic society should we cease to tolerate those who abuse the benefits of tolerance and perhaps threaten the survival of democracy? At a more mundane level, what kind of behaviour (for example, unkindness to pets) must not be tolerated as a matter of taste, but condemned as offending against another important value or belief?

Once again, it has to be stressed that I am not recommending that every school should have 'belief system' on the timetable, and appoint suitably qualified staff to teach it. But it is not sufficient to say that this is part of the hidden curriculum or 'we teach it all the time'. Schools must first of all map out the conceptual territory and the related 'experiences' and then find out how they will be covered within the existing subject areas; if gaps are identified by this process, then someone must be given responsibility for planning the coverage. Technical details about how this may be accomplished will be included in chapter 6. There will also be some overlap between some of the concepts involved – for example, the difference between power and authority – and the kind of curriculum already recommended above under the 'social system' discussion of Crick and Porter (1979). There will also be overlaps with the moral system.

8   The aesthetic system

Another kind of confusion exists in the aesthetic system. Teachers are unclear and uneasy about attitudes to 'high culture' and 'popular' or 'mass culture'. This is not a problem which can be completely solved, nor is it desirable that it should be, but far greater attempts need to be made to clarify what the issues are in terms of aesthetic criteria and judging what is excellent rather than to accept the total confusion as inevitable.

Schools also offer too limited a range of aesthetic experiences: painting and drawing may be available, but other media need to be fostered such as sculpture, pottery and photography. Many schools still teach woodwork and metal work as 'skill subjects' rather than exercises in design, where aesthetic criteria could be discussed and developed. It will be important to give pupils as wide a range of short-term options (or 'tasters') as possible in order to establish particular skills and talents, but no one should be permitted to opt out of the aesthetic curriculum altogether. The Gulbenkian Report (1982), *The Arts in Schools*, contains a useful critical review of this area.

Schools also tend to focus on the aesthetic modes of the past rather than the contemporary media; for example, novels and plays will be present in the curriculum, but film and television studies are likely to be ignored or sadly neglected. There is also a tendency to divorce aesthetics from everyday life. Many opportunities exist within subjects already on the timetable, and much could be achieved by rethinking the basic principles involved.

The next stage of the analysis or curriculum plan will be concerned with comparing the eight systems with the content of existing school subjects; it will then be necessary to see how those subjects could be developed or complemented by additional subjects so that a more comprehensive common curriculum might be developed. It will always be an advantage for teachers to have opportunities for in-service training of various kinds, but the basic principle being pressed at this stage of the analysis is that teachers' subject specialisms should not be undervalued in the process of curriculum reform. One of the major errors of 'curriculum development' in the 1950s and 1960s was to encourage ideas such as 'integrated humanities' which often resulted in good history teachers spending half their time teaching mediocre or inaccurate geography. The purpose of encouraging teachers to rethink what they have to offer from the basis of their own subject specialism is that they should no longer teach, say, history as history, but would also need to ask 'what does history have to contribute to the pupil's understanding of one of the eight systems suggested as the basis of the cultural analysis?' In this way some gaps can be filled and mismatches avoided.

In the next chapter, the question of matching the cultural needs with the subject specialisms of the teaching staff will be examined in much greater detail. The key to success in this process of adjustment is to make maximum use of teachers' talents: they are frequently underestimated. There are some gaps which are aggravated by a shortage of teachers (for example, design technology), but in most cases the existing teaching force could do a much better job if they were given the opportunity of planning a better curriculum along the lines suggested.

Summary

Before proceeding to chapter 6, it may be useful to summarise the 'gaps and mismatches' identified by this stage of the cultural analysis:

1 Political and social education is frequently lacking or inadequate.
2 Economics should be part of the common curriculum, rather than an option.
3 The Bullock Report should be looked at again, not just used as an excuse for more reading tests. 'Communication' is wider than 'language'!
4 Science and mathematics teaching need radical reform, including becoming less abstract and more meaningful; other 'subjects' to be seen as different kinds of 'truth'.
5 Technology should be part of the common curriculum; its status as a subject improved and related to other subjects.
6 A rational policy for secular morality needs to be developed and made part of the common curriculum.
7 Schools cannot be value-free; values and beliefs should be clarified and incorporated into a common curriculum.
8 All young people have aesthetic needs; 'the arts' should be seen *not* as peripheral but as an essential part of the curriculum for all pupils.

All of these gaps and mismatches need to be taken account of nationally, but some of them will be more appropriately remedied as part of school-based curriculum planning. This will be considered in chapter 6.

NOTES

1 DES/HMI (1978); DES/HMI (1979); Rutter, M. L. *et al.* (1979).
2 See Dr Robert Stradling (1977); also Crick and Porter (1979).
3 The Assessment of Performance Unit (APU) of the DES originally proposed (B. Kay, 1975) that tests should be constructed to cover work across the whole curriculum – not subject by subject. Eight lines of development were put forward in the Kay model, one of which was social and personal development, but this was later dropped from the testing programme. (See Lawton (1980) for a full account of the APU.)
4 See materials of the Schools Council Project *History, Geography and Social Science 8–13*; also Lawton, D. and Dufour, B. (1975).
5 See Barnes, D. *et al* (1969) for the 'mismatch' between teachers' language and the pupils', and Stubbs, M. (1976) for a wider discussion of language and schools.
6 There is a further difficulty in the case of poetry (and English literature generally) which does not apply to art or music. Although the basic appreciation of a poem is not 'scientific', there are aspects of poetry appreciation (or, for example, 'understanding a novel') which does rely on the collection of 'evidence' and discussing its importance – just like some kinds of scientific problem. The problem remains, but is even more complex than suggested in chapter 5.
7 Both John White (1973) and Robert Dearden (1972) have put forward persuasive arguments in favour of moral autonomy. In a democratic society it is essential that young people not only 'do the right things' but internalise the reasons for doing them. A true democracy requires not obedient citizens but questioning adults equipped with sets of principles rather than 'right answers'.
8 Many comprehensive schools organise 'registration' each morning and afternoon not in age-group classes, but in all-age groups with a tutor, one of whose duties is to get to know all members of his group. In some schools time is allotted to the tutor group either on a daily basis or perhaps twice a week for general administration. In some LEAs it is also quite common for the tutor to have a responsibility for the 'moral education' of his group using project materials of various kinds. See publications from Schools Council Moral Education Project, including *Lifeline* packs, and McPhail *et al.* (1972). See also May (1971).

6 School-based Planning for a Common Curriculum

Prophets may teach private wisdom;
teachers must deal in public knowledge.

Lawrence Stenhouse*

Detailed curriculum planning must be the responsibility of teachers themselves within a particular school. Some general principles can be laid down as a basis for translating national guidelines into a working curriculum, but no attempt will be made to construct *the* curriculum for *all* schools. Nevertheless, it may be useful at this stage to look at the problem of replanning the curriculum from the point of view of a school. In order to make the case realistically difficult, let us imagine a very traditional secondary school. If it were a primary school, many of the same principles would apply, but the organisational task would be much easier. Since the school is so traditional, the curriculum is organised in terms of school subjects with easily recognised titles (no nonsense about faculties and integrated humanities here!).

Twelve subjects (table 1) appear on the timetable including Craft, Design and Technology (CDT) and Home Economics (which used to be for boys and girls respectively, but since the sex discrimination legislation both have become available for all). All twelve subjects exist as a common curriculum for Years 1 to 3, but then a complex core and option system takes over for Year 4 and the 16+ examination Year 5.

---

* (1975) *An Introduction to Curriculum Research and Development.*

Table 1

Existing subjects in Secondary School

a English (E)
b Mathematics (Ma)
c Science (Sc)
d Religious Education (R)
e History (H)
f Geography (G)
g French (F)
h Art (A)
i Music (Mu)
j Physical Education (PE)
k Craft, Design and Technology (CDT)
l Home Economics (HE)

How could such a school begin to adapt to the kind of requirements laid down as a result of the curriculum analysis in chapters 3 to 5? Two kinds of problem arise at this stage: the first is epistemological – including the question of covering the ground adequately; the second is organisational – the research literature on curriculum innovation has provided a good deal of vicarious learning experience about how to ensure the continued cooperation of teaching staff at a time of organisational change.[1] In this chapter, I am mainly concerned with the question of curriculum coverage, but the second issue is so closely related that it should be considered at the same time.

A superficial glance at table 2, which compares existing subjects with what is needed in terms of the eight systems, might give the impression that the conversion to a cultural analysis type of curriculum would be very easy: surely most history teachers have sufficient knowledge of political theory to construct and teach a respectable course on politics which is required for System 1? Similarly, are there any religious education teachers who know so little about ethics that they could not cope with what has been suggested as necessary for System 6 and moral education?

Table 2

	Systems	Existing Subjects	New Subjects or Topics Needed	Comment
1	Social and	History Geography	Politics Economics	
2	Economic		Sociology	
3	Communication	English	Communication Studies	
		Modern Languages Mathematics	Film & TV Studies	
4	Rationality	Science History Mathematics English		All subjects
5	Technology	Craft, Design and Technology Science History Home Economics	Microtechnology Computer Studies	
6	Moral	Religious Education	Comparative Religious Studies Ethics	Link with 1/2
7	Belief system	History Religious Education	Politics	Link with 1/2
8	Aesthetic	Art Music English Literature Home Economics Physical Education	Film & TV Studies	

To take that view might be over-optimistic unless certain dangers were observed and precautions taken. The two immediate dangers would be: first, that the traditional curriculum might survive and the extensions to it be so minimal as to make no real difference; second, teachers might pay lip service to the new curriculum, but carry on almost entirely in the old tradition. The evidence of research literature is that the major obstacle to be overcome at this stage is the tendency for teachers to want to retain the security of what they have been doing prior to the 'reform'. Teachers may indeed feel threatened by the prospect of change. To overcome this difficulty, teacher involvement at all stages of planning is vital. Major problems cannot be solved by a committee structure, but a sensible policy of teacher involvement by means of committees may be an essential prerequisite to successful planning.

It has been suggested (Lawton, 1973) that three levels of discussion in committees might be useful. The first level would be concerned with general balance and coverage for the whole curriculum, and should be chaired by the head teacher or a director of studies or curriculum co-ordinator if one had been appointed by this time. The purpose of this committee would be to seek the co-operation of all departments in planning the whole curriculum. If it were thought that a committee of twelve departmental representatives plus a chairman were too large, then some possible regroupings might be made. For example, history plus geography, English plus modern languages, art plus music, and so on. But great care should be taken to ensure that every department feels that they are represented on this important planning committee.

The second level of committee work is concerned with maximum co-operation and co-ordination *within* departments, or if regroupings are beginning to take place, within the new larger departments. The organisation of level 2 would simply be departmental committees with the departmental head as chairman. Finally, level 3 committee discussions would be concerned with inter-departmental integration to ensure maximum co-operation and co-ordination between departments. This would consist of two kinds of meetings: (a) full staff meetings to review and discuss co-operation; (b) *ad hoc* groupings of two or more departments who wish to co-operate on specific tasks.

Table 3   A Possible Committee Structure

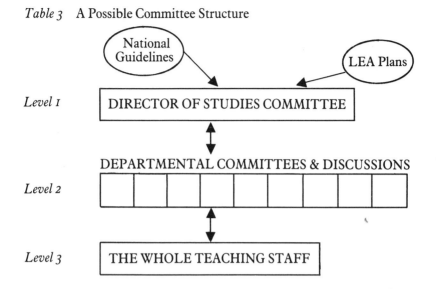

The object of the three-level set of committees and discussions is to ensure that all members of staff are involved and feel that they are involved, and have a real opportunity for voicing their own particular points of view. Provided that this principle is observed, then other possible structures might meet the needs of particular schools better than what has been proposed above. Experience has shown, however, that much planning time must be made available and timetabled. This kind of planning exercise simply cannot be fitted in to lunch hours and coffee breaks. All sorts of informal arrangements might be made as well, but it is essential to have a formal committee structure to undertake the very considerable task of replanning.

The first task of any level of committee would be to discuss the reasons for changing the curriculum. In my experience, no group of teachers who begin to look at their own school curriculum from the point of view of cultural analysis will continue for long to be satisfied with the status quo.

The second task would be to examine possible curriculum models to get beyond subjects. Once it is recognised that subjects are means not ends in the teaching process, then some 'super-subject model' becomes necessary. For some schools my eight systems cultural analysis model might be too remote, and an intermediate model might be helpful. There might be some political advantage, for example, in adopting the HMI eight areas of experience model from *Curriculum 11–16* (1977) which has the additional advantage of being known to be a success – at least in some areas (HMI, 1981).[2]

At this stage it might also be appropriate to have discussions about other models such as Hirst or Phenix, and to look at the general problem of the structure of knowledge into subjects or disciplines. There may even be suggestions at this for much more radical solutions such as complete abolition of subjects and a totally 'integrated curriculum'. Experience of the 1950s and 1960s, however, would encourage caution here. The loss of the subject specialisation of the teachers is probably greater than the gains from a fully integrated curriculum.[3]

Some discussions of subjects and disciplines will now become necessary, not least to preserve the self-confidence of specialist teachers. A very common explanation of subjects is that school timetables are organised with examinations in mind, and examinations have been set in terms of conventional school subjects. But this is a very poor justification for subjects. We are frequently told that examinations should follow the curriculum rather than dictate it, although the reverse is more commonly the case. A school which is replanning its curriculum, however, will have the opportunity of making examinations the servants rather than the masters.

How can subject divisions be justified? The first point is that I would want to accept Lawrence Stenhouse's statement that whereas prophets may deal in private wisdom, schools must be concerned with public knowledge. Public knowledge in western societies has been organised into subjects or disciplines: they are man-made not God-given but they affect our thinking in powerful ways. Another way of looking at the function of school in the transmission of knowledge is to accept Bernstein's division of knowledge into common sense knowledge and non-common sense knowledge; schools must be concerned with various kinds of *non*-common sense knowledge. If we add to that distinction the notion that education is concerned with good sense not common sense, then we are perhaps on the way towards making curriculum concerned with good sense, but related to pupils' common sense view of reality. To take Bernstein's distinction a little further it would be necessary to say that the curriculum is concerned with various kinds of 'good sense' and it is the task of pedagogy (or the craft of the teacher) to relate good sense in the form of subjects or disciplines with the child's own view of reality acquired through personal experience. Subjects may be 'artificial', but they provide a useful means to more important ends – so long as the curriculum is not dominated by them.

Another item on the agenda for a school curriculum committee would be to work at a policy for the whole curriculum in terms of a common curriculum, including the vexed question of options for the 14-16 age-group.

A number of independent researchers such as Hurman (1979) and Reid (1974), as well as HMI (1977) and (1979), have all come to the conclusion that the typical 'core plus options' structure for the 14+ age-group is a very poor substitute for a properly planned curriculum. The arguments against options may be summarised as follows: the choice given to pupils is more apparent than real – many pupils do not get what they choose; when pupils do get what they choose the result is often a badly unbalanced curriculum or a curriculum with serious gaps – girls tending to opt out of mathematics and science, for example; choices are often made for inadequate reasons – wanting to stay with friends or to avoid a particular teacher; from the school point of view, option choices are frequently used as hidden devices for selection – that is, the purpose is organisational rather than educational.

In view of this kind of evidence, HMI in *Curriculum 11–16* made a strong plea for a 14+ curriculum which would emphasise the kind of knowledge and experiences that all young people ought to have access to, and which would take up about three-quarters of the time available, leaving a much smaller amount of time for option choices than is now customary in England.

What is meant by common curriculum in this context? Should it be distinguished from compulsory curriculum (which has an unfortunate ring)[4] and a uniform curriculum?

Earlier chapters of this book have been concerned with the question of culture, and the fact that even in a complex, pluralist society there must be a common culture (as well as regional and other sub-cultures which are also important). Much of chapter 4 was concerned with looking at one society, England, and analysing its common culture with a view to selecting from that culture in order to provide guidelines for a school curriculum. It was also noted that in England the 1944 Education Act made secondary education free and compulsory for all pupils from the age of eleven up to the compulsory leaving age at present. That Education Act is also the legislative force behind the strong cultural attachment to social justice or fairness which implies that education is one of those important areas in a society where equality of opportunity should prevail. After a brief experiment with tri-partite arrangements[5] of schools, whereby children were selected at 11 for 'different but equal' secondary schools, comprehensive arrangements were accepted as national policy for secondary education.[6]

Comprehensive schools themselves went through a three phase evolution. At first, most of them became tri-partite systems within the school: pupils were streamed into classes on the basis of 'measured ability' in various ways and thereafter followed different curricula. A second phase followed a questioning of this internal segregation and began to experiment with more flexible, less permanent forms of separation such as 'setting' for a few subjects only, and in some schools, mixed ability grouping on a much wider scale. The third phase was concerned with the content of the curriculum and its comprehensiveness in terms of reaching all pupils. This phase was still in progress when the debate on curriculum became public in 1976.[7] The most important question in the early 1970s was: 'What is the point of a common, comprehensive school unless it transmits a common culture by means of a common curriculum?' Two further questions emerged from this evolutionary process: first, what kind of common curriculum? Second, how is it to be organised so that no pupil is denied access to worthwhile knowledge and experiences, and no pupil is held back from achieving his greatest potential?

It is at that point that our imaginary secondary school has begun to consider the problem of curriculum planning, and it will probably be necessary for the staff to be reminded both of the historical facts – at least as far back as 1944 and preferably further – and of the nature of the debate surrounding comprehensive schools in general and the common curriculum idea in particular.

It may also be important at this stage to dispel certain misconceptions about the common curriculum. First, it should not be confused with the policy of having a uniform curriculum. It would be impossible, even if desirable, to ensure that all pupils learned exactly the same amount from any teaching programme. But that should certainly not be the intention in any case. The common curriculum idea requires that teachers work out the major ideas, concepts and experiences which will give access to worthwhile knowledge (widely defined) and make this minimum programme available to all pupils. It should be understood that some pupils will go much further, some will leave the basic understanding of the common programme very far behind. But all pupils will have been given access to, for example, real science and real history, not the 'Mickey Mouse' alternatives to knowledge which are sometimes provided for so-called less able children.

The second distinction which should be made is that the idea of a common curriculum does *not* involve central direction of the curriculum. There are arguments in favour of achieving a greater degree of professional consensus on the content of the secondary curriculum – the 1977 Green Paper, for example, talked of 'acceptable and unacceptable kinds of diversity' – but there is no reason why this should mean that the curriculum should be directed from a central authority such as the DES. There would seem to be some advantages of having certain agreed guidelines laid down nationally – say, by the Schools Council as in the *Practical Curriculum* (1981), or by another body on which professional interests are in a majority position; and there are advantages in having a degree of co-ordination regionally (in England by LEAs), but the detailed planning of curricula must be carried out by teachers working in their own schools.

Are there any helpful points of advice which might be given to our team of secondary teachers in just that position?

In any situation like this we are faced with teachers who have been trained and socialised within the school for one curriculum model (the traditional subject approach) and 'matching' them with the demands or needs of a different model – the cultural analysis model. The 'content', previously thought of as needing no justification, other than being necessary for passing examinations at sixteen or eighteen, now needs to be seen as a means to a more general cultural end. More specifically, teachers need to think of their subject or discipline in terms of a new set of goals – perhaps the cultural analysis approach and its eight cultural systems or possibly an intermediate model such as the 'Areas of Experience' in HMI *Curriculum 11–16*.

Matrix Planning

A curriculum planning technique which is very useful for coping with this complex matching process is the curriculum matrix. Essentially the curriculum matrix is a means of comparing existing resources with a new specification, identifying gaps (and possibly mismatches) and thus enabling a better set of programmes to be planned. A sensible strategy is to start at the most general and all embracing (Matrix A or B), and then progressively to refine the process so as to match subject offerings with curricular needs on a year by year basis.

Table 4   Matrix A

Purpose: to match existing subjects (teachers) with the requirements of the new curriculum, identifying 'gaps'.

Existing subjects	a E	b Ma	c Sc	d R	e H	f G	g F	h A	i Mu	j PE	k CDT	l HE

Systems (including new subjects)

1   Social
    (politics)
    (sociology)

2   Economic
    (economics)

3   Communication
    (communications studies)
    (film/TV)

4   Rationality

5   Technology
    (micro)
    (computer studies)

6   Morality
    (comparative)
    (ethics)

7   Belief

8   Aesthetic
    (film and TV)
    (sculpture)
    (photography)

Table 5 Matrix B

Purpose: to match existing subjects with the new curriculum using
HMI *Curriculum 11–16* Areas of Experience Model.

Existing	a	b	c	d	e	f	g	h	i	j	k	l
subjects	E	Ma	Sc	R	H	G	F	A	Mu	PE	CDT	HE

Areas

1 Linguistic

2 Mathematics

3 Science

4 Aesthetic

5 Ethical

6 Social and Political

7 Spiritual

8 Physical

Thus the sequence of events for a school staff could be as follows:
1 Select a curriculum model (for example, sub-dividing knowledge or experiences in some meaningful way), as suggested in
   Curriculum 11–16 Areas of Experience Model (table 5, Matrix
   B) or Lawton's eight systems (table 4, Matrix A).
2 For each area of experience (assuming *Curriculum 11–16* has
   been chosen) groups of teachers (possibly, but not necessarily,
   in departments) must move towards syllabus construction by
   mapping out the knowledge territory – in some cases perhaps
   by listing knowledge (concepts), skills and attitudes to be
   covered by the end of the programme; then breaking this
   content down into five separate years.
3 Achieving a rough matching of existing subjects (and teachers)
   with the new requirements. See table 4 (Matrix A) or table 5
   (Matrix B).
   This will identify major gaps, so that, for example, it may be
that no department can identify a teacher who feels confident to
offer elementary economics. If this is the case, then a managerial

decision is necessary – can someone be retrained or will a new appointment be needed?

4   Having identified (and eventually filled) major gaps in provision, we now move to more detailed matrix analysis. Each year, every area of the curriculum must be matched against subject offerings: for example, Year 1, Political Education, see table 6 (Matrix C).

Table 6   Matrix C

Purpose: to match existing subjects with the requirements of the new Political Literacy Curriculum.

Subjects:	History	Geography	English	Religious Education	
Political Concepts:					
power					
force					
authority					
order					
law					
justice					

It will be seen that this detailed matching process will necessitate a total of at least forty detailed matrices (5 years × 8 areas of experience = 40 matrices; but some areas may be sub-divided). In each case existing subject departments (or individual teachers) will be asked: 'What can you offer in terms of, for example, "authority" as a concept?' Further gaps may then be identified – and filled.

By this process existing programmes and syllabuses can be modified and adapted to meet the newly defined needs of the pupils in terms of access to the different 'areas of experience'. Teachers' subject expertise is not threatened, but is extended and made the most of. It will, of course, also be necessary to ensure that these departmental 'offerings' add up to a coherent programme from the pupils' point of view. This must be a serious responsibility for a reasonably senior member of staff. But beware bureaucracy – it is teachers' attitudes that matter most!

It is also unrealistic to expect schools to plan the whole of the curriculum themselves from first principles. They need to look for and discuss the merits of 'second-hand' models, and then see how they can best co-operate to achieve certain goals or cover the ground most effectively. For example, I have already indicated that in most schools one of the most sadly neglected areas is that of political education. We have a general aim of understanding politics and the political structure under our System 1 (social system). If the group of teachers in our school were to attempt to work out a five-year syllabus from scratch, as non-experts they would find it extremely difficult, time-consuming and would still probably produce only a mediocre programme with serious omissions and possibly some errors. It so happens, however, that a distinguished political scientist, Professor Bernard Crick, is very interested in political education in schools, has devoted many years to devising a programme for 'political literacy', and has discussed it with teacher colleagues. Some aspects of the programme have been tried out in schools (see Crick and Porter, 1979). So the sensible course of action for our group of historians and geography teachers who, we shall say, are well-meaning but not well-versed in political education, would be to *begin* by looking at the programme for political literacy and seeing to what extent it might serve *not* as a syllabus, but as a basis for their own syllabus building.

Crick (1979, page 62) suggests, for example, the following as a conceptual approach to political literacy:

By the age of sixteen all young people should have an understanding of all concepts in table 7 and the networks of relationships between them. Having accepted this scheme, it would

Table 7

TABULAR SUMMARY

GOVERNMENT

POWER	FORCE	AUTHORITY	ORDER
(the ability to achieve an intended effect either by force or more usually by claims to authority)	(physical pressure or use of weapons to achieve an intended effect – latent in all government, constant in none)	(respect and obedience given by virtue of an institution, group or person fulfilling a function agreed to be needed and in which he or it has superior knowledge or skill)	(when expectations are fulfilled and calculations can be made without fear of all the circumstances and assumptions changing)

RELATIONSHIPS

LAW	JUSTICE	REPRESENTATION	PRESSURE
(the body of general rules made, published and enforced by governments and recognised as binding the government even if not as just)	(what is due to people as the result of some process accepted as fair irrespective of the outcome)	(the claim for the few to represent the many because they embody some external attribute, of which popular consent is only one of many)	(all the means by which government and people influence each other, other than by Law or by Force)

PEOPLE

NATURAL RIGHTS	INDIVIDUALITY	FREEDOM	WELFARE
(the minimum conditions for proper human existence – prior even to legal and political rights)	(what we perceive as unique to each man and to mankind – to be distinguished from individualism, and purely 19th century doctrine)	(the making of choices and doing things of public significance in a self-willed and uncoerced way)	(the belief that the prosperity and happiness of individuals and communities is a concern of government, not merely mere survival)

then be for our team of teachers to decide how their own subjects – history, geography or whatever – could be utilised to ensure that over a five-year period the basic learning could take place so that the majority of pupils would have gained some experience of discussing and understanding the key concepts. This would not be to suggest, of course, that history and geography would have no purpose other than encouraging political literacy, only that this arrangement would provide an additional purpose which might involve changes in both content and style of teaching. For example, almost any period in history would lend itself to discussions of 'power' and 'authority', but a change in emphasis might be needed from the history teachers' usual approach – or it might not be.[8]

Similarly, a group of religious education teachers might be well advised not to attempt to work out a programme in elementary ethics or moral education from first principles, but should look for possible models.[9] Such a process of curriculum planning not only involves rethinking individual subjects, it will also involve looking *beyond subjects*, and developing patterns of co-operation with other departments. For example, English teachers may have a good deal to offer in both politics and moral education. Many English teachers already are proud of the contributions which they make in one or other of these fields. But if they are to be truly effective the 'English' offerings would need to be co-ordinated with the moral or political contributions made by other subject departments. Some schools have, following the ideas in *Curriculum 11–16*, appointed co-ordinators for such difficult cross-subject areas as political education, technology or social studies. This is often found to be more effective than attempting to create new subjects and squeeze them into a timetable. A co-ordinator of this kind needs to be responsible not only for the co-ordination of the teaching, but also an evaluation of the learning.

Curriculum planning at the school level is to some extent a complex matching operation: matching national guidelines (which, it is to be hoped, will have been agreed upon after careful process of cultural analysis) with local needs and resources. Above all, planning at this level will be concerned with matching curricular requirements with what existing teachers can offer with or without retraining. It might be said that this is exactly what happens in many secondary schools at the moment: if no physics teacher is available physics is dropped from the timetable; no money to employ a part-time music teacher – drop music! Few would want to justify that kind of negative 'planning', however.

The 'matching' process I am advocating is based on the assumption that all children have a *right of access* to certain kinds of worthwhile knowledge and experiences which have been selected by cultural analysis. If a teacher does not already exist for an important subject or area of experience then one must be found or retrained. But access for the pupils *must* be provided. That is one reason why national guidelines can be an advantage.

Departmental planning

Having worked out a policy for the whole curriculum in general terms, teachers can then turn their attention to departmental planning which is often also somewhat neglected in many schools. At this stage curriculum planning is concerned with syllabuses: that is, in secondary schools, programmes of a more or less detailed kind covering the five-year 11–16 period (or whatever the period of years covered happens to be). There may well be departmental differences in the level of detail which must be stipulated: an English teacher might resent being given a list of poems to be covered, year by year, whereas a science teacher will find it much easier to accept a more detailed teaching syllabus. But in all departments discussion will be appropriate, and as much agreement as possible is desirable. There will always be room left for teacher autonomy in the classroom – that is not really the problem, although it is often seen as the problem when curriculum planning is discussed. It may also be important to point out at this stage that questions of sequence in curriculum planning are not entirely arbitrary. Bruner (1966) invites teachers to apply the 'shuffle test' to the sequence of their teaching programme – if changing the sequence of presentation makes no difference perhaps it should! There are logical and psychological advantages in some patterns of order rather than others. In science and mathematics some of these are very obvious, but the question should always be asked as part of the professional planning of courses. In addition, of course, there are questions of 'readiness' often raised in the context of Piaget's stages of development.[10] Bruner has also put forward the notion of the spiral curriculum as of possible merit in some educational contexts.[11]

The next kind of planning to be undertaken by a department (or teaching group) will be the need to prepare a variety of approaches, materials and other resources to meet the need of different kinds of pupils. The most obvious categorisation here is to talk of able and less able pupils; even to cater differently in this way would be an advance in many schools, but there are other differences as well. It is surprising that after so many years of work in educational psychology so little is done about differences in 'learning style'. Teachers often talk about pupils being 'introverts' or 'extroverts' but rarely make any concessions to the different approaches to teaching and learning which might be desirable. And there are other categories of pupil personality or perceptual type which teachers should plan to take into consideration.

What this means in terms of curriculum planning is that a syllabus should be thought of not simply in terms of content or experiences to be made available, but in terms of the need to provide different kinds of access for different types of pupil. The 1938 Spens Report mistake was to say that because pupils are different, they must have different kinds of curriculum; it would now seem more appropriate to suggest that teachers must try to accommodate different kinds of pupils by providing varieties of approach or access to a *common* curriculum.

Whilst it is true that in any subject any class, however carefully selected, will be a 'mixed ability group', this does not allow us to escape from a major problem of organisation in comprehensive schools, which is to offer a common curriculum to a very wide range of abilities and learning style. It is necessary for schools and departments within schools to think out the problem and to establish a policy. At school level it would seem to be acknowledged that it is difficult to reconcile the principles of comprehensive education (including a common curriculum) with a pattern of organisation which would rigidly segregate pupils by ability at a very early age. For this reason many comprehensive schools have adapted the policy of mixed ability groups for Years 1–3 (11–14 age) and then a structure based on 'setting' rather than 'streaming'.[12] This leaves a number of organisational issues to be settled at departmental level: how to avoid teaching to the middle (thus boring the 'quick' and bemusing the slow); how to ensure that individual differences are catered for within the common curriculum whilst preserving essential content and sequences for all. In some subjects, it is much easier – in mathematics, for example, there are several schemes available whereby the same essential content is covered, but pupils are guided through more or less material, difficult or easy problems, by means of colour coded routes. In other subjects it is not quite so clear, but solutions are always possible. For example, in a first year's work on 'Man and Society', it might be considered useful to begin with a study of 'Animal Societies'. If so, a possible teaching plan might consist of the following:

(a) *Common course* for all pupils:
Relate the following concepts to bees, ants
and primates – territory
communication
ritual
division of labour
inter-dependence
reproduction and
    rearing offspring

(b) *Optional*:
More detailed work on *either* bees *or* ants and/or primates using books and worksheets, but without whole-class lessons

(c) *More difficult option*:
  (i) worksheet on *animal communication* based on reading chapter 2 of G. Barry's *Communication and Language*, and/or
 (ii) worksheet based on reading *Man and Monkey* by L. Williams, and/or
(iii) worksheet based on reading *In the Shadow of Man* by Jane Goodall

(NOTE all three books in (c) are worthy of being read by first year secondary pupils and would be interesting in their own right, but it is important that 'optional' tasks are not seen as 'silent reading' but result in some kind of permanent record of work which can be evaluated.)

Thus for this section of a first term's work (five or six weeks?) some pupils will tackle only (a), some will do (a) and (b), others will complete (a) and (b) and (c). But all will have covered the essential concepts and reached some understanding of them. After the basic work has been completed, choice comes into question, gently guided by the teacher's knowledge of an individual pupil's reading skills and other abilities. What should be avoided is the notion that the 'able' can go off and read a book about monkeys while the 'less able' draw a picture of a monkey! Every time a choice is given the teacher should be confident that each option is 'worthwhile' and 'productive' in terms of a child's development, conceptual or otherwise. No activity which is merely 'time-filling' is justifiable.

Such pre-planning as suggested above is time-consuming but certainly repays the effort involved (especially if it is a co-operative departmental responsibility), and it should be regarded as a normal requirement for a professional teacher. School-based curriculum planning is not simply concerned with the 'whole curriculum' – much neglected though it is: it is concerned with planning a sequence of meaningful learning experiences for all children in the school.

Part of the answer is that teachers need to think of their 'schemes of work' in much more flexible ways than teaching a series of lessons to thirty pupils who all learn the same thing at the same pace. Each department in our imaginary school will need to think out strategies and alternative approaches. It might be, for example, that those concerned with social and political education would plan as follows:

1   Make a list of topics, or questions to be explored and generalisations to be encouraged which *all* pupils should encounter by the end of the programme. This selection would embody the 'conceptual structure of the discipline' as well as a list of appropriate content. It is effectively the common curriculum for that subject area.

2   The most appropriate *sequence* should be worked out, year by year, term by term. (Let us suppose twelve topics for Year 1.)

3   For each topic, provide additional topics or themes (as in the example on Animal Behaviour given above). This supplementary list should cater for differences in ability as well as offering choices based on interests. Diagrammatically possible sequences can be mapped out as follows:

Table 8

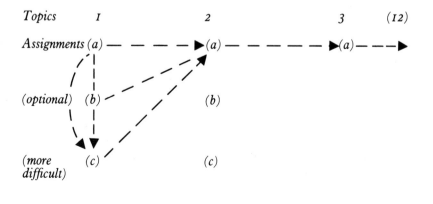

Records of Progress

It would be important to keep adequate records of each pupil's path through the assignments, with some evaluation of the conceptual development involved. It should not be assumed (and

Table 9

Topic 1   Animal Behaviour
            Date started:
            Date completed:

Concepts:	territory	communication	ritual	division	interdependence	r + r
Assignments						
(a)	S 10/9	G 11/9	S 10/9	S 11/9	S 12/9	G 12/9
(b) bees ants primates	G 4/10	G 5/10			G 4/10	
(c) communication man and monkey chimps						G 8/10

[NOTE Indicate S (some grasp), G (good understanding) for each concept after each assignment is completed. Please date each entry and make a note of any particular points you think should be recorded.]

records will show this) that the most 'able' are the quickest: some pupils have a facility for rushing through work with very little understanding. Another aspect of the teacher's skill is to be able to slow down some pupils by making greater demands on them without lowering their motivation.

In the case of our set of assignments for Topic 1 on Animal Behaviour described above an acceptable record sheet for each pupil would look something like table 9.

The above example of a topic is ambitious in attempting so many 'new' concepts (6 or 7 is probably too many) in one topic. But it is a less complex recording operation than some in the area of social and political education where 'attitudes' and 'skills' would have to be recorded in a similar way. A more typical record might be arranged as shown in table 10 – restricting the number of concepts to a more manageable number but including some attitudes/values and skills.

Once again what must above all be avoided is a bureaucratic attitude towards such records, either taking them off mechanically or pretending that they are more meaningful than they really are. They can, at best, be no more than *systematic* notes of teachers' impressions; at worst they are time-wasting bits of paper. Which category they fall into will depend on teachers' attitudes. If teachers are involved in the curriculum planning, stage by stage, and if they are involved in the design and planning of the evaluation-record sheets, then they will tend to treat the process seriously; if they see the records as something imposed on them by an ambitious deputy head or head of department they are more likely to pay only lip-service to the innovation.

It has often been said that there can be no curriculum development without teacher development. But that does not necessarily mean sending teachers away for courses on curriculum studies: very often the best kind of curriculum development and teacher development is school-based.

It is now clear from research such as Rutter *et al.* (1979) that planning at school level does make a difference to pupils' achievement. Pupils perform better in a school atmosphere where there is a sense of purpose and order, and where teachers co-operate rather than work as complete individualists. Brian Simon (1981) has, partly in this connection, pointed out the curious lack of attention paid to 'pedagogy' in England – that is attempting to see teaching and learning as a single, interactive process rather than two separate activities. There is considerable scope for discussions of

Table 10

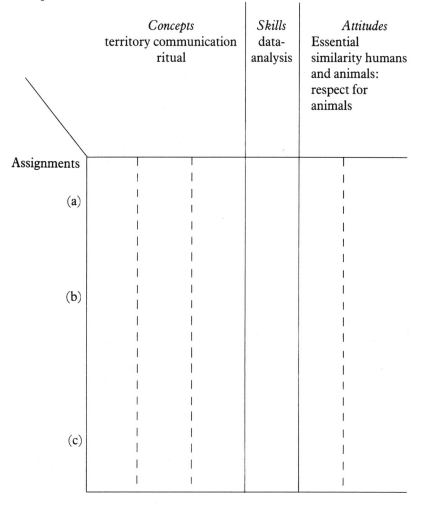

Topic 1   Animal Behaviour

	Concepts territory communication ritual		*Skills* data- analysis	*Attitudes* Essential similarity humans and animals: respect for animals
Assignments				
(a)				
(b)				
(c)				

curriculum and pedagogy within every school; once again a possible objection to this is that to have a school policy on certain aspects of teaching methods and teaching style would be to limit the autonomy of the teacher, but this is to take too narrow a view of the range of choices open to individual teachers. For example, if a school history department decided to adopt the Schools Council

13–16 history project, this would involve a commitment not only to using certain kinds of material, but also to a style of teaching which would give pupils a more active role in judging the value of certain kinds of evidence. This is certainly a very different kind of 'history' from notes dictated for memorisation, but does not make the teachers either superfluous or their role completely uniform: there is still plenty of scope for teachers to 'be themselves' within a rather different teaching situation.

Similarly, it will be necessary for teachers – at school level and departmental level – to agree policies on evaluation, testing and record-keeping. Traditional schools already have a policy on such phenomena as yearly or half-yearly examinations, but even these, where they still exist, are not adequate instruments for evaluation of pupils' progress; too often they are a substitute for professional evaluation and records rather than a fulfilment of a sensible academic policy – a ritual to be gone through once or twice a year, sometimes conscientiously, sometimes cynically with comments such as 'could do better', but rarely effectively and professionally. Adequate classroom evaluation and record-keeping would relate individual pupils' 'profiles' much more closely to details of the syllabus being taught, identifying specific strengths and weaknesses in mastery of particular skills and concepts rather than very vague and general comments.

One weakness in many schools is that pupils themselves are inadequately informed of their own strengths and weaknesses. Pupils' work is 'corrected' and 'marked' but any indications given of quality tend to be normative rather than individually diagnostic: a pupil may be informed that he is below average but is unlikely to be given specific assistance in how to master a particular difficulty.

Another surprising omission in many schools is a policy for coping with periods of pupil absence. Very often it is simply assumed that somehow a pupil will 'catch up', but no formal arrangement exists for being given help. Too much is left to informal arrangements; if no adequate system of recording progress exists as well, serious gaps may persist in a pupil's knowledge. The idea of pupils being to some extent responsible for their own evaluation is dependent on adequate feedback from the teacher. This is not to suggest that pupils should be responsible for their own curriculum planning – quite the reverse. It is merely to suggest that pupils need to be more involved in their own progress, and that this can best be achieved by meaningful interaction between teacher and pupil rather than two distinct operations. Many schools do suffer (as Rutter *et al.* demonstrate) from pupil alienation, in the sense that the work pupils are asked to do has no real 'meaning' for them, and in no way 'belongs' to them. A mistaken diagnosis of this problem often results in trying to make school work 'relevant' to the lives of the pupils; the real problem is to make pupils care about their work by feeling that it is theirs – even if it is very abstract and remote from their experience of everyday life.

Summary

Curriculum planning at school and departmental levels should involve all teachers. They need to discuss possible planning models and then translate general aims into syllabuses. Curriculum matrix analysis may be a useful, even if time-consuming, technique for identifying 'gaps and mismatches'. Finally, teachers need to work together to develop improved techniques of evaluation and record-keeping in the context of each school's curriculum policy.

NOTES

1 Marten Shipman (1974) gives a number of useful examples, including the fact that a head teacher alone can produce little effective change. Macdonald and Walker (1976) also give some useful advice on curriculum innovation.
2 As a follow-up to *Curriculum 11–16*, HMI invited a small number of schools in three LEAs to 'try out' the new kind of common curriculum based on 'areas of experience'. The generally encouraging results of that development are reported in *The Secondary Curriculum 11–16: A Report on Progress* (1981).
3 The theoretical and practical problems of a 'fully integrated curriculum' are discussed in Richard Pring (1976). See also Reynolds and Skilbeck (1976).
4 John White's book *Towards a Compulsory Curriculum* (1973) is, in my view, a convincing justification for the idea of a common curriculum, but is *tactically* wrong in referring to a compulsory curriculum. It might be agreed that there are some kinds of knowledge or experience which are so important that schools should be compelled to offer

them, but in terms of pupils, persuasion is always likely to be preferable to compulsion.

5 There are some exceptions: some areas – notably Anglesey and London – were committed to comprehensive education from the beginning.

6 It would be wrong, however, to give the impression that no controversy now remains about comprehensive education. The Conservative Party has always had doubts, and perhaps the most obvious example of this equivocal attitude is the 'assisted places scheme' which is designed to 'cream off' the brightest pupils and send them to independent schools.

7 In 1976, James Callaghan, Prime Minister in the Labour Government, made a speech at Ruskin College, Oxford, which was the beginning of a 'Great Debate' on education. The curriculum of primary and secondary schools was an important feature of the debate.

8 Similar procedures could be adopted for covering other aspects of the social system using, for example, Lawton and Dufour (1975) or Whitehead (1979) for the economic system. If it were possible to provide extra time, say, one period a week for Years 3 to 5, then a book such as my *Investigating Society* (1979) might provide a co-ordinating role to the approach already suggested. See also Alex Porter (1982) for a further discussion of political literacy.

9 For example, the materials prepared by Leslie Button (1981–2) or John Wilson (1971). See also the discussion of moral and religious education in the volume in this series by Edwin Cox (1983).

10 Most teachers are familiar with Piaget's work on stages of development (sensory-motor, pre-operational, concrete operations, formal operations). But this is often interpreted negatively – especially in the context of 'readiness' – rather than positively by asking 'what should a teacher be doing to make the child ready for . . .?' See Lawton, D. (1981) for a further discussion of Piaget.

11 Bruner's notion of the 'spiral curriculum' would fit in particularly well with the kind of planning envisaged in this chapter. The spiral curriculum is based on the view that difficult concepts need to be introduced not once and then assumed to be understood, but several times in carefully placed contexts.

12 'Setting' is usually taken to mean put into ability groups for a minority of the timetable and perhaps one or two subjects only; whereas 'streaming' means making a general decision to categorise a pupil in all subjects.

7 Accountability and Curriculum Evaluation

> Evaluation entails a view of society. People differ about evaluation because they differ about what society is, what it can be and what it ought to be. Much of the debate about evaluation is ideology disguised as technology.*

Since Ralph Tyler's book was published in 1949 it has become customary for any book on curriculum to include a section or chapter on evaluation, variously defined. Since the mid-1970s, however, curriculum in England has also been linked with questions of accountability. Since the connection is far from obvious, it might be useful to begin this chapter by establishing some of the possible relationships.

Evaluation is essentially concerned with supplying information about the success or failure of a teaching-learning situation, whether it is feedback of marks to pupils after a test, or a teacher coming to a conclusion about the need for a new approach next year, or the results of a GCE 16+ examination or – most complex of all – the formal, written report on a new curriculum project to those who provided funds for it. Each of those situations is different in purpose and methods used, but in each case a judgement is made about the performance of teachers or pupils, or the 'value' of the methods or materials being used.

Accountability is concerned with responsibility and acknowledging that responsibility in some public form. Accountability is, of course, a metaphor derived from the world of industry and commerce, and there are many educationists who doubt the wisdom of using the term in educational contexts. There may be some resemblance between the responsible teacher and the managing director accountable to company shareholders at the end of

---

* (1977) HAMILTON, D. *et al.*, *Beyond the Numbers Game* (Introduction).

the year, but the differences may be even greater – as we shall see later in this chapter. The person who is accountable has to demonstrate success (or acknowledge failure) in some way which is publicly meaningful: he is evaluated by others in terms of the evidence presented. Accountability, therefore, involves evaluation, but evaluation does not necessarily entail accountability.

Accountability

Accountability as an educational concept was imported into England from the USA during the 1970s. It is relevant to sketch its history in America first. Lessinger (1971) traces the use of the term 'accountability' in educational contexts back to the late 1960s in the USA. But the tradition from which this usage was derived is much older (see chapter 2 of this book). Callahan (1962) claims that business values and practices were being adopted in educational administration in the States soon after 1900, and school administrators were tending to identify with business executives rather than with scholars and educational philosophers. The culture of the USA is, according to Callahan's analysis, dominated by the world of business and by the business ethic; not only do American businessmen earn more money than academics, they enjoy higher social status and prestige; given the choice, educational administrators readily identified with the values and practices of the world of business rather than scholarship. By 1907 there were clear indications that aspects of business ideology had reached the classroom; a key book was *Classroom Management* by W. C. Bagley, which saw school management as a 'problem of economy', and discussed this problem in terms of 'plant' and return on investment; classroom management was simply a business problem involving investment and dividends.

The work of Franklin Bobbitt has already been referred to in chapter 2: typical of his early publications was *The Elimination of Waste in Education* (1912); his influence on school supervision was considerable especially through the National Society for the Study of Education. Bobbitt's policy was to apply business efficiency and factory organisation to schools; this entailed adopting standards and measurement scales so that results could be reported in quantitative terms. Bobbitt realised that the task was not an easy one, and that it would require a system of *accounting* which would be more elaborate than that of a factory or a railway, but which was essential for 'efficient management, direction and supervision' (Callahan, 1962, page 85). Bobbitt's policy was never completely accepted but it certainly left its mark on the American school system. During the 1960s, the United States' social climate was again more favourably disposed to efficiency and scientism[1] (see House, 1975 and Atkin, 1979).

When Lyndon Johnson became President of the USA in 1963 he was so impressed with Robert MacNamara, who had introduced to the Department of Defense the managerial techniques of The Ford Motor Company, that he ordered other government departments to adopt the same business efficiency methods. These methods included management by objectives, cost benefit analysis, systems analysis and planned programmed bugeting.

Between 1965 and 1967 a series of seminars was held to encourage administrators in education to learn from the Department of Defense. Crude input and output models were applied to schools. Behavioural objectives became a major part of these efficiency systems and accountability projects in the 1960s. Some educationists protested that schools were concerned with goals that went beyond those that could be stated in behavioural terms, and that behavioural objectives were undesirably limiting. Such views were generally ignored, and those who held them were considered to be old-fashioned and unscientific.

In some cases, the efficiency methods developed into large scale accountability projects. One of the best known was the Michigan State Accountability System. This plan stipulated objective tests for all fourth and seventh graders in Michigan. A second stage of the plan involved cash awards to schools on the basis of gains in achievement test scores. Test scores were also made public, published in newspapers and compared with scores in other schools.

Although the plan was not universally condemned by educationists, the 80,000 teachers in the Michigan Education Association were very critical. In 1973, The National Education Association (NEA)[2] became concerned that the plan might spread to other states. An independent evaluation of the plan was commissioned. This evaluation (House, Rivers and Stufflebeam, 1974) criticised the way the goals had been derived, the construction of the tests, the lack of participation by teachers as well as a number of technical points. The debate continued for several years (see E. House, 1978). The point that clearly emerged from the debate was that conflict was inevitable between the values of business efficiency and what teachers regarded as good practice in schools.

In England the growth of 'accountability' as a term has been associated with a number of factors: general disenchantment with education; the deteriorating economic situation; the growth of consumerism and parent power; as well as specific loss of confidence in some schools such as the William Tyndale scandal.[3]

Accountability often means more testing, or the publication of examination results and the consequent growth of a league table mentality. Such practices have been deplored by teachers' professional organisations and other educationists in the UK (see Lacey and Lawton, 1981), but important theoretical objections to the educational implications of accountability have also been registered.

Sockett (1980) has attacked the usage of the term 'accountability' on grounds of lack of clarity regarding 'accountable to whom?' He suggests that it could be argued that teachers should be accountable to individual pupils and parents; pupils and their parents as part of the community; a teacher's employers, for example, the LEA; the providers of the resources, both LEA and government; professional peers, that is, other teachers, inside and outside school; other relevant educational institutions, for example, universities and other types of school; the public, industry and the trade unions.

According to Sockett such a list is far too diffuse to be satisfactory. It is, however, unlikely that teachers will be allowed to escape from accountability simply because there is so much ambiguity about the meaning of the word and its applicability to various groups. It is true that the pattern of accountability described by Sockett is more complex than a company director being responsible to a group of shareholders, but that does not destroy the analogy altogether. Company directors are 'accountable' to their own employees, tax inspectors, other government agencies, as well as to shareholders. Rather than dismiss the accountability metaphor altogether, it may be more prudent to examine it carefully and qualify it in a suitable way for educational purposes.

Along these lines, a very useful distinction has been made by Eraut (1981) between the moral, the contractual or legal, and the professional accountability of teachers. All citizens have an obligation to obey the law of the land, but a teacher is, in addition, legally accountable to his head and the LEA employing him, and *only* to those two legally. A teacher has no contractual relationship with either pupils or parents. But he does, of course, have a moral obligation towards them, which might be seen as a kind of 'accountability'. This moral obligation to pupils may be stronger in a teacher's view than any legal contract that he has.

The same distinction can be made for a head or a chief education officer. A head is legally accountable to his governing body and to the LEA, but morally accountable to his teachers, pupils and parents. Having made this distinction between legal and moral accountability, Eraut then goes on to make a most important point, namely, that schools are right to observe that the accountability relationship with the LEA involves mutual obligations, 'but should not conclude that the relationship is symmetrical by confusing legal with moral accountability' (page 147).

Eraut's third form of accountability is concerned with teachers' claims to be professionals.[4] The arguments put forward by teachers to justify the claim for professional accountability are concerned with professional expertise, training and the maintenance of standards and values professionally, and professional autonomy. This kind of professional autonomy and accountability is, of course, complicated by overlapping to some extent with contractual arrangements. But the claims for professionalism have not been generally accepted. Teachers do not have a professional code of practice, and it would be difficult to achieve agreement about what competent teaching involves. If there is consensus about certain kinds of incompetence, only the most extreme cases are acted upon.

It is also ironic that as the educational qualifications of the general public improve, there must be a diminishing of reliance on 'subject' knowledge as a justification for professionalism, and an increase in the importance of the 'professional' knowledge of how to teach and how to plan a worthwhile curriculum. But most secondary school teachers are lacking in those kinds of knowledge on which their professionalism is increasingly going to rest.

Maclure (1978) had earlier made an equally useful sub-classification in terms of the four main concerns associated with accountability: standards, curriculum content, parental participation and managerial responsibility. These four aspects of accountability are also discussed by Eraut (1981).

Under the heading 'standards' Eraut makes the interesting and valid point that much of the public debate about standards is 'irrational'. Judgements about schools are seldom based on available evidence; opinions are formed from fragments of personal experience and from 'eulogistic reflection on the past'. An interpretation of evidence is influenced by 'lay theories of education' incorporating ideas like a fixed pool of talent, rote learning and the early appearance of giftedness. Part of the explanation for this would seem to be that every member of the public has had experience of schooling, and he tends to base his 'expertise' on this very limited experience. So, if the teaching profession is itself conservative, then the public at large will be even more conservative. From the point of view of cultural analysis this is very important and must be taken into account, but not allowed to dominate planning.

One of the dangers of the 'standards' debate, as seen by both Maclure and Eraut, is the tendency to give tests and testing too much prominence. Eraut concludes his discussion of standards with the telling remark that in the context of testing 'there remains the uneasy feeling amongst teachers that all schools will somehow be expected to be above average!' (page 151).

Accountability applied to curriculum content will tend to emphasise three aspects: first, more attention to basic skills; second, examination results and threats to publish league tables; third, pressure to make the curriculum more vocational and emphasising links between schools and industry. Once again, I would stress the fallacies of these views in terms of the purpose of education as portrayed by a cultural analysis. As we have seen, cultural analysis demonstrates clearly that much more is needed from the school curriculum than the very narrow view of 'useful knowledge' implied in many recent discussions about curriculum content.

Maclure's third category in the accountability debate was 'parent participation'. In many respects, this is a direct challenge to teacher professionalism. Parents – or rather some groups of parents – since the 1960s have demanded various rights including the right to discuss curriculum. But there is a contradiction in arguments about parental involvement in school government. Such arguments are often based on the desirability of community participation, but as Eraut points out, choice implies a lack of commitment to any individual school and is associated with the market approach to accountability which is the opposite of a community approach. Eraut sees no way out of this dilemma so long as the education system serves as a mechanism for distributing qualifications. Those who possess qualifications have a vested interest in preserving their currency. Educational planning based on cultural analysis should, therefore, seek to minimise this 'examining' function in schools as well as the 'job-selecting' function.

Maclure's final category of the accountability debate is 'managerial responsibility'. Eraut comments that what to the insider appears to be a reasonable compromise between interested parties, often appears to the outside as endless opportunities for 'passing the buck'. This was illustrated only too clearly by the William Tyndale affair. With curriculum as with other aspects of administration there is no clear demarcation between national, LEA and teachers' responsibilities. This lack of clarity may be exploited by teachers on some occasions, but when crises arise, teachers then become extremely vulnerable to attack from outsiders. This kind of division of responsibility also needs to be seen as part of a cultural analysis approach to curriculum planning and school organisation.

A final point might be made on accountability before proceeding to the closely related question of evaluation. Both Sockett and Eraut have pointed out the complex nature of accountability. Yet it continues to be used as though it were a very simple process. I would like to suggest a distinction between bureaucratic accountability and democratic accountability. Much public discussion of accountability is in terms of one way 'upward accountability', that is, the responsibility of a subordinate to give an account to a superior for money spent, resources used, and so on. But I would suggest that kind of bureaucratic accountability especially in the light of Eraut's distinction between 'legal' and 'moral', would be inappropriate in education. Here, what is required is a much more complex pattern which I would refer to as democratic accountability. This would be a two way process: the teachers are accountable to pupils as well as to the head teachers or the inspector; the head teacher is accountable to his assistant teachers as well as to the governors and the LEA. This may be shown in an over-simplified way by the following two diagrams:

Figure 4

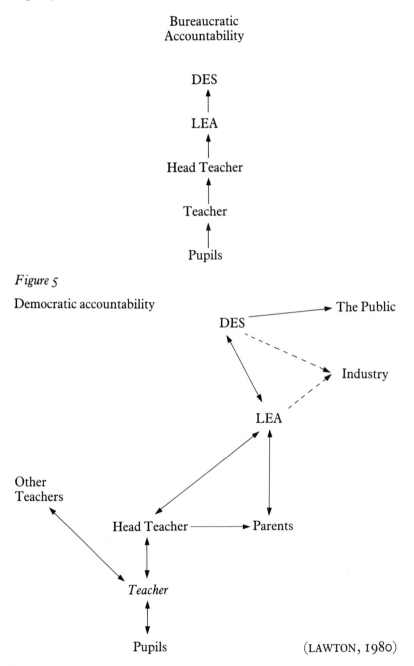

Bureaucratic
Accountability

DES
↑
LEA
↑
Head Teacher
↑
Teacher
↑
Pupils

Figure 5

Democratic accountability

The Public

DES

Industry

LEA

Other
Teachers

Head Teacher ⟶ Parents

Teacher

Pupils

(LAWTON, 1980)

Evaluation

Evaluation, like accountability, is by no means as simple an issue as it often appears to outsiders. In some respects, as we shall see in chapter 8, evaluation – like accountability – is a political activity (see House, 1973). Evaluation involves decisions about efficiency, the purpose of education, teaching methods, as well as the means of collecting evidence and coming to conclusions about all these. One dilemma is that evaluation is a complex and difficult process requiring expertise, but accountability seems to demand public discussion of 'results' and the methods involved in getting the results: there is a tension between 'the right to know' and the difficulties of meaningful presentation of information to non-experts. There are at least seven kinds of evaluation which are necessary from time to time in most educational systems:

1   Estimates of pupil progress and/or competence.
2   Estimates of pupil competence at the end of schooling.
3   Estimates of teacher competence for various purposes, includ-
    ing promotion.
4   Judgements about the efficiency of a school (or group of
    schools).
5   Methods of providing useful information about teaching
    materials, including new curriculum projects.
6   The evaluation of diffusion or dissemination.
7   Underlying all these is another kind of evaluation often
    ignored, but really the most important of all: judgment about
    quality of the process involved (that is, is what the pupil is
    learning, or the teacher trying to teach, *worth while?*).

The first four kinds of evaluation listed above have been accepted 'traditionally' as necessary functions in any educational system: it is important to *know* that schools and teachers are reasonably efficient, and that pupils (or a reasonable percentage of them) are learning something. Various methods have been used to make these kinds of judgements, and there has often been some controversy about the advantages and disadvantages of different methods. For example, in England the early inspectors were confident of their ability to make good judgements on an impressionistic basis – they felt that they knew a good school when they saw one! But after the Newcastle Report (1861), this method was called into question, and HMI were required to test pupils according to 'standards' laid down centrally. Many inspectors, including Matthew Arnold, disliked this method intensely, partly because it imposed rigid criteria and a restricting effect on the curriculum. The teachers too were far from enthusiastic about the method of evaluation, and the early history of the National Union of Teachers (NUT) was mainly concerned with fighting against this kind of inspection and the testing involved.

More recently, a similar debate has arisen concerning category 5 above – that is, evaluating materials or curriculum projects. Is quality best judged by setting tests of pupil achievement or by more impressionistic methods? Or by a combination of the two? Because large sums of money have been invested in some curriculum development projects, the question of effectiveness in terms of 'value for money' became an issue; this gave rise to evaluation as a kind of educational growth industry with groups of professional evaluators possessing their own language and conflicting views on methodology.

This debate about the evaluation of curriculum development projects is not only interesting in its own right, but has additional importance in terms of school and classroom practice. There has been a tendency for the methods (and arguments about the methods) used by professional project evaluators to spill over into the first four kinds of traditional evaluation. One of the purposes of this section will be to attempt to 'demystify' the current arguments among professional evaluators and to see what relevance these debates have for school and classroom evaluation.[5] Both in terms of teaching efficiency and good manners towards pupils, teachers should be able to provide useful feedback on progress. It also seems to me that many teachers do not take this aspect of their job sufficiently seriously, or perhaps lack the professional skills necessary to do it properly. In most schools – primary and secondary – there is room for improvement in assessment techniques and record keeping. But more large scale testing, either by the APU or by LEAs,[6] is unlikely to improve the situation.

There is, however, much to be learned from discussions about curriculum development project evaluation (category 5) if teachers can cope with the more esoteric aspects of the evaluation debate. I have elsewhere (Lawton, 1980) suggested a six-fold analysis of evaluation models. The models are 'ideal types' rather than exemplars of actual practice:

1   the classical (or agricultural botanical) research model;
2   the research and development (R and D) (or industrial/factory) model;
3   the illuminative (or anthropological) model;
4   the briefing decision-makers (or political) model;
5   the teacher as researcher (or professional) model;
6   the case study (or portrayal) model.

Model 1: Classical (or agricultural-botanical)

The classical model treats the problem of evaluating a curriculum project or a teaching style as the same kind of research as an experiment in agriculture or botany. An agriculturalist tests the efficiency of a new fertiliser by (a) measuring the height of the plant; (b) applying the fertiliser; (c) measuring again after a suitable time lapse; (d) comparing the growth of the experimental plant with that of plants in a control group (no fertiliser applied).

According to this model, an educationist would:

(a)   test two groups of pupils on a specific part of the curriculum;
(b)   apply the new teaching technique in one of those groups;
(c)   test again;
(d)   compare the learning in the experimental group with the results in the control group pupils.

This should indicate whether the programme in the experimental group is superior or not to that in the control group which had not been exposed to the new programme. Statistical tests can be applied to see whether any difference is significant or not.

This may sound plausible, but it ignores the fundamental difference between human beings and plants, namely, that human beings perform differently when under observation whereas cabbages do not. The unintended consequences of human observation are likely to be much more important in the educational situation.[7]

There are also technical difficulties involved in this kind of experimental research. With a class of children there are usually too many variables involved to produce a neat experimental design such as the agricultural example. The researcher must either have extremely large samples to even out the possible differences involved, or have very strict controls which raise ethical questions.

If you really know or think you know that method (a) is better than method (b), is it morally justifiable to submit any children to method (b)? Another technical difficulty is that there is a tendency to concentrate on *average* differences between the control group and the experimental group, and to ignore the important *individual* differences. The larger the group (and therefore the better from some statistical points of view), the greater the pressure to neglect individuals.

Another difficulty is the exaggerated importance given to test results. There is a tendency for experimenters to measure what can be easily quantified. (It is easy to test whether a child has remembered a list of dates in history at the end of the year's programme; it is much more difficult to assess whether that child is likely to be interested in history in ten years' time – but surely that is what history teachers really want?)

Finally, this kind of experiment is often based on a fallacy. The assumption is made that the same subject matter is being taught to the experimental group as to the control group, but in a different way or using different materials. This is not necessarily so; for example, it is not possible to evaluate new mathematics by giving tests of traditional mathematics. In other words, new mathematics is not simply a better way of teaching old mathematics: it is a different kind of mathematics, and it would be grossly unfair to apply a test of old mathematics in both cases. Tests are often used and interpreted as though they were not 'problematic', but they nearly always are. The tests themselves make various assumptions about teaching and the kind of content which is involved.

Model 2: Research and development (or industrial/factory model)

Some would see this model as essentially a variation of the classical model, but in my view there are very important differences.

According to this model, all curriculum development should begin with research, one result of which would be a clarification of the goals. The industrialist must know exactly what he is trying to produce; the school must know what kind of differences in pupil behaviour will be achieved. We should note the similarity between this model of evaluation, and the Bobbitt approach discussed in chapter 2 and earlier in this chapter.

The task of 'R and D' evaluation is five-fold:

(i)   translate agreed aims into specific, measurable behavioural objectives;

(ii)   devise appropriate learning experiences;

(iii) devise tests to assess student performances;

(iv) administer tests with a sample of classes using the new programme;

(v)   process results to yield useful information to the team which is producing the new programme, or to the sponsors and potential users of the project.

Control groups might be used, but they might be avoided for reasons given under Model 1.

There remain a number of objections to this kind of evaluation in addition to those outlined under Model 1:

(a)   As we have seen, there are theoretical as well as practical difficulties in translating aims into pre-specifiable behavioural objectives.

(b)   This means that the task of testing is made more difficult than it would first appear – perhaps impossible in some cases.

(c)   The difficulty of finding representative samples is enormous. There are too many variables.

(d)   The culture of the school is ignored, so are individual differences of teachers and pupils.

In England, several Schools Council projects started on the basis of objectives, but moved away from the rigidity of that model (*Science 5 to 13* is the obvious example and has been written up in detail).[8] Outside England, one of the best known examples was the Swedish IMU Mathematics Project. This was very carefully researched, but the problem of *unintended consequences* eventually became apparent. Pupils' boredom, the dissatisfaction of the teachers who did not like their role and political use of the project were all unforeseen at the beginning, but became enormously important by the end of the project.

Model 3: Illuminative (or anthropological)

This tradition has a reasonably long history, but it received detailed theoretical attention in a now famous paper, 'Evaluation as Illumination' (1972) written by Parlett and Hamilton. This paper not only represented a reaction against classical and R and D models, but was, in a positive way, a move towards anthropological methods of evaluation. Stress was also placed on the complexity of educational evaluation and the need for 'general illumination' rather than specific test results.

This view has met with some sympathy, but the problems involved in illuminative evaluation have not been entirely solved. Rules of procedure are not yet sufficiently clear and accusations about subjective impressions are not entirely unfounded. Another problem which emerged with the 'new wave' evaluations[9] was the development of esoteric methods and language which tended to make evaluation even more remote from teachers and administrators than conventional research.

The importance of this kind of evaluation in terms of cultural analysis is that it represents a move away from narrow psychological views of teaching and learning and sees the classroom as part of a complex cultural situation.

Model 4: Briefing decision-makers (the political model)

Cronbach (1963) suggested that evaluation should not only be concerned with providing information about the success of teaching or learning, but with information about which decisions have to be made. Barry MacDonald, in England, has carried on in that tradition and developed the decision-making model in an interesting way. According to MacDonald (1976) evaluation is inevitably concerned with power in education. He has outlined three 'ideal types' (bureaucratic, autocratic and democratic evaluation) and suggests that the style of an evaluation must be related to a particular political stance. Evaluators cannot escape that political involvement and should stop pretending that they are value-free. MacDonald rejects the view that evaluation is the task of making a judgement about the success of an educational programme; he states that it is a very complex process of collecting information (including judgements) which will enable the decision-makers to make a more rational choice.

Evaluators must know what type of evaluation they are likely to be involved in and negotiate a contract accordingly. The three 'ideal types' of evaluation are:

(a) **Bureaucratic evaluation** which is an unconditional service to those government agencies controlling educational resources. The evaluator accepts the values of those holding office (the administrators) and provides information to help them accomplish their policy objectives. His role is that of a management consultant; his criterion of success is client satisfaction; his report is owned by the bureaucrats; in return for a fee he gives information and advice and has no responsibility over ultimate decisions.

(b) **Autocratic evaluation**. This style of evaluation involves *conditional* service. The evaluator provides external validation in exchange for strict compliance with his recommendations. Values are derived from the evaluator's perception of the constitutional and moral obligation of the administrators. The focus is upon issues of educational merit; the role of the evaluator is expert. The techniques of study must be seen as yielding scientific proofs because the evaluator's power-base is the respectability of the academic research community. His contract must guarantee complete non-interference; the evaluator retains ownership of his (her) report. (The evaluator is the 'autocrat' in this model.)

(c) **Democratic evaluation**. An information service to the whole community. Sponsorship by one group (for example, the administrators) does not give them a special claim to advice or secret information. The assumption behind this model is 'value pluralism' – there is no consensus about basic values. The only value which can be assumed is the desirability of an informed citizenry. The role of the democratic evaluator is that of 'an honest broker'. The report must be written so that it is accessible to non-specialists. It must offer confidentiality to informants. The evaluation report will be non-recommendatory. Since this model is essentially concerned with the problems of professional evaluators, it probably has least to offer practising teachers trying to improve their own assessment techniques.

Model 5: Teacher as researcher (the professional model)

Stenhouse (1975) suggested that evaluation should move away from the product and process models[10] of curriculum towards a research model. He refused to accept the distinction between evaluation and research and instead cast the teacher/developer/researcher in the role of investigator. The curriculum the teacher creates will not be right or wrong, but will be judged by whether it advances knowledge or not. It is a probe through which to explore and test hypotheses, not a recommendation to be adopted.

According to this model the teacher is a professional indulging in 'research-based teaching'. Evaluation must be 'self-evaluation'.

One of the problems here is that of role conflict: the teacher has to be both someone to encourage learning, and also the participant observer trying to assess success and failure in the classroom. Some of the research which has developed out of this notion has attempted to deal with that problem.[11] The great merit of this approach is that the culture of the school and the culture of the classroom retain their significance.

Model 6: Case study (or portrayal model)

Many of the illuminative or new wave evaluators have stressed that they wish to retain, where appropriate, some of the traditional methods of measurement including survey, check lists and questionnaires. But they wanted to use such 'hard data' only where it was appropriate, and wanted to rely on other more impressionistic methods as a basis for their whole study. This eclectic approach is sometimes referred to as case study which implies a modified version of illuminative evaluation (although Parlett and Hamilton also stressed that they did not wish to reject all traditional methods). There has been a good deal of work on case study methodology. (See, for example, a report on the Second Cambridge Conference (December, 1975) written by Adelman, Jenkins and Kemmis, 1976.) Case study data is often said to be 'strong in reality but difficult to organise'. The 'portrayal' version of this model owes much to the work of Bob Stake[12] who advocates a mixture of measurement and anthropological methods.

Evaluation and Cultural Analysis

What is the relevance of these six models of evaluation just discussed to the kinds of evaluation needs I outlined at the beginning of this chapter? Clearly, cultural analysis has more in common with evaluation models 3–6 than the first two; the idea of matching models to the specific cultural needs is a general principle to be observed.

It is sometimes asserted that one of the advantages of the Tyler objectives model of curriculum is that evaluation is built into the system as a prominent and inescapable feature of curriculum development; it is certainly one of its attractions as far as many administrators are concerned. On the other hand, the cultural analysis approach might be said to be strong on justification, but apparently weak on evaluation. This is not necessarily the case: I suggest that cultural analysis procedures should be applied at every stage of the model and at every level of evaluation. It may be useful to demonstrate this by returning to the seven kinds of evaluation which, at the beginning of the chapter, I asserted would be likely to appear in any national system of evaluation; I will then apply the criteria of cultural analysis to the particular problems which arise.

Evaluation Type 1: Estimates of pupil progress or competence

Before devising a test or other assessment instrument, the teacher must ask certain prior questions:

(a) Is the learning really worth while? (If not, do not test it – drop it!)
(b) How important is the learning intrinsically (that is, in its own right)?
(c) How important is it sequentially (that is, how essential is it in the wider context of past and future learning?)?
(d) What are the most important features of what has been learned (for example, memorisation of facts compared with understanding concepts or generalisations)? If concepts are what the teacher really wants to stress, he should not test memorising facts simply because that is easier to test.
(e) How can I best devise an effective assessment instrument (that is, effective in terms of feedback to pupils, and a basis for future learning)?
(f) How can I convert assessment into a useful record of progress?

This may seem to be a tall order for a teacher every time a classroom test is applied, but such sequential questions (and others) can soon become second nature to a professional teacher. There may also be ready-made 'aids' available, which need not be disregarded simply because they might appear to look too much like behavioural objectives – they can often be adapted: for instance, the following kind of matrix in economics might be taken as a model for a variety of teaching/learning situations:

Table of Specifications for a 50-Item Test on a
Unit in Economics (Money and Banking)

	Instructional Objectives			
	1	*2*	*3*	*4*
Content Areas	*Knows Basic Terms*	*Understands Concepts and Principles*	*Applies Principles*	*Interprets Data*
A Forms and functions of money	3	4	3	
B Operation of banks	4	3	5	3
C Roles of the Federal Reserve System	4	6	3	2
D State regulation of banks	4	2	4	
Total number of test items	15	15	15	5

(Lawton and Dufour, 1973, page 61)

In this way, class evaluation becomes not an afterthought to the teaching process, but an integral part of the planning and record-keeping.

Evaluation Type 2: Estimates of pupil competence at the end of the school period

In most countries there is some kind of school leaving certificate which is given to pupils on completion of a compulsory period of schooling, although different societies attach more or less importance to this and use different methods of assessment. England is peculiar in several ways: first, great importance is paid to this event for the more able, but less academic pupils may leave school

without any kind of certificate; secondly, because so much importance is attached to the academic testing it is not entrusted to
teachers in their own schools, but is a 'public' or external examination; thirdly, in the UK the 'examination tail tends to wag the
curriculum dog' more than in most other countries.

In terms of cultural analysis the existing 16+ examination
structure is a nonsense. If someone wanted to invent a pattern of
assessment specifically designed to alienate the majority of pupils,
it would be difficult to improve on the current system of GCE 'O'
level and CSE examinations. The present arrangements are not
only offensive to the idea of a common curriculum, but are even
damaging to the needs of the economy in terms of crude manpower
planning. Minimally, a structure of assessment needs to be designed which will not only include all pupils at sixteen, but will
avoid classifying large numbers of young people as failures long
before they reach the end of their compulsory period of schooling.
The present proposals for a common system of examinations at
16+[13] may go some way towards improving the worst aspects, but
not far enough; some of the ideas for a profile of achievement are
more promising, but there are also dangers here which will need to
be avoided if cultural analysis principles are to be applied.

Evaluation Type 3: Estimates of teacher competence

Eraut (1981) has pointed out that one of the difficulties at the
moment is that consensus about teacher effectiveness and competence is lacking. This consensus may never be totally achieved in a
pluralistic society, but use of cultural analysis would at least clarify
both what teachers ought to be teaching and what are regarded as
appropriate methods. What can be ruled out, for reasons which
have been discussed already, are crude systems of payment by
results whereby teachers are judged in terms of the performance of
their pupils on standardised tests, or any variations of the American systems of 'performance-based teacher evaluation'.

In recent years there has been some movement in the direction
of school-based teacher evaluation and teacher self-assessment.
These methods are of some interest (see Maurice Holt (1981) for
criticisms of them), but they are probably more useful for improving teachers' professionalism than for judging competence.

Evaluation Type 4: Judgements about school efficiency

Crude measurements in terms of standardised tests and public examination results are completely inadequate, and often very misleading. But it may be that many schools are too bureaucratic and narrowly focused to provide appropriate learning environments. Cultural analysis methods would suggest that it is necessary to look at schools in a broad way and to establish goals on a wider scale than preparation for employment. Becher (1979) suggests that schools should be allowed to establish for themselves what kind of school they wish to be and then to be judged by appropriate criteria on a peer assessment basis. This is interesting, but could be dangerous if crude market pressures were allowed to prevail – what if most parents wanted schools to train their children for jobs? It is important to look at the question of school efficiency not simply from one angle – the parents' point of view – but from a variety of cultural viewpoints; a complete cultural analysis is required. Methods of school self-evaluation with external moderation are, however, likely to be of more value than simple measures of efficiency based on testing.

Evaluation Type 5: Evaluation of materials and curriculum development projects

I have already indicated the complexity of this task in my review of the six evaluation models (pages 100–5 of this chapter). From the point of view of school-based curriculum planning there are at least two separate issues: first, deciding whether to adopt a particular project or set of materials; second, the evaluation of a project when it is in use after adoption.

The first can best be accomplished using the curriculum matrix approach outlined in chapter 6, the major issue being whether the project makes a worthwhile contribution to the school curriculum. Many projects have been adopted for unsatisfactory reasons – for example, because they are 'in fashion' or have been recommended by an inspector.

The second kind of in-school evaluation of a project might be assisted by using a very simple flow chart:

Evaluation: A Suggested Sequence of Questions

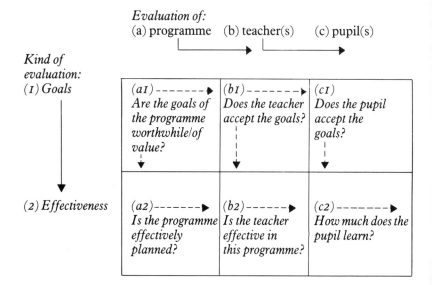

Evaluation of:
(a) programme   (b) teacher(s)   (c) pupil(s)

Kind of evaluation:

(1) Goals	(a1) --------▶ Are the goals of the programme worthwhile/of value?	(b1) -------▶ Does the teacher accept the goals?	(c1) Does the pupil accept the goals?
(2) Effectiveness	(a2) -------▶ Is the programme effectively planned?	(b2) ------▶ Is the teacher effective in this programme?	(c2) -------▶ How much does the pupil learn?

Evaluation Type 6: Evaluation of dissemination and diffusion

In the early years of the Schools Council in England, for example, it was thought that the process of diffusion[14] would proceed without any deliberate effort: good ideas would gradually be taken up and used by rational teachers. By the early 1970s, this was clearly not happening, and the Council began to concentrate a good deal of attention on the theory and practice of dissemination. It remains a major problem which is clearly a 'cultural' one. Increasingly dissemination has been concerned with national networks such as teacher's subject associations, and local networks such as teachers' centres. Some work has been done of a theoretical nature, but much more is necessary. There is now some evidence to believe that it would be a mistake to 'write off' the centre-periphery[15] model completely. What is needed is a much more sensitive analysis of the periphery and the links between centre and periphery.

Evaluation Type 7: Worthwhileness

I have elsewhere (Lawton, 1973) attempted to analyse Richard Peters' (1966) philosophical approach to worthwhileness and to incorporate it into a curriculum plan. It was not entirely successful; nevertheless the problem of categorising some activities as worthwhile (and therefore of educational importance) cannot be ignored. I began my description of cultural analysis with the assertion that some aspects of any society's culture must be judged by reference to values which are not limited to that society but are in some sense cultural invariants. In terms of cultural analysis and curriculum planning worthwhileness must be treated in that way.

Peters' attempt to justify 'worthwhile' curriculum activities rests on four criteria. The first is connected with time: a worthwhile activity will be capable of holding interest for a long period. The second is that a worthwhile activity should not impede other kinds of worthwhile activities and should not conflict with other principles such as ethical and aesthetic. Third, worthwhile knowledge (such as science) illuminates the world outside itself whereas a trivial activity (such as golf) is not open-ended in that way. Finally, a worthwhile activity is non-competitive: gaining knowledge about literature does not prevent others from giving knowledge, whereas collecting books does prevent others from owning those books – knowledge acquisition is worthwhile in a way that collecting 'things' is not.

There are, as I indicated above, certain problems with the Peters view, but there is enough here, in my view, to justify the use of the concept 'worthwhile', and teachers would do well to think of their own teaching (and curriculum planning) bearing these criteria in mind; evaluation without an understanding of worthwhile activities would be meaningless.

We need constantly to remind ourselves that evaluation is concerned not simply with measuring performance, but with improving performance by evaluating the whole teacher/learning context. This will involve 'valuing' as well as measuring. Seen in this way, accountability as well as evaluation takes on a quite different light. Since a judgement about 'value' can only be made within some kind of 'value-system' or 'belief-system', the very wide implications of educational evaluation should always be recognised.

Summary

Both 'accountability' and 'evaluation' are extremely complex and politically dangerous concepts. The relation between them needs careful analysis. Accountability in education should be seen as a democratic two-way process rather than an aspect of hierarchical control. Evaluation – carefully defined – is a necessary part of curriculum planning, but is also susceptible to political abuse. The two concepts should be seen in the wider context of cultural analysis.

NOTES

1 Scientism is a word frequently used in this context as well as a criticism of a more general attitude: it is used to describe the view that the methods of the natural sciences are the *only* source of knowledge, and must be applied to man and society.

2 The NEA is the largest teachers' union in the US.

3 See the Auld Report (1976) for details of the William Tyndale School's problem.

4 Eraut suggests that teachers' claim to be professionals is complicated by confusion between personal accountability and colleagual accountability – a confusion which is sometimes deliberate.

5 I would accept many of Maurice Holt's (1981) criticisms of evaluation in schools, but I could not agree entirely with his view that teacher professionalism is a substitute for evaluation.

6 The Assessment of Performance Unit (APU) and the national testing programme will be discussed in chapter 8. One accusation made against it is that not only has it produced tests itself but has encouraged LEAs to 'overtest'.

7 See Note 1 above. This is all part of the same debate: are human beings just as 'predictable' as cabbages – if only we knew the 'laws'?

8 See Schools Council *Evaluation in Curriculum Development* (1973).

9 Many evaluators who would appear to fall into the 'illuminative' category object to being given this title. A more general term is 'new wave' which includes all those not committed to Models 1 or 2.

10 Stenhouse (1975) rejected the product model of curriculum (that is, one based on 'outputs' specified as behavioural objectives) and also discussed the advantages of the process model as a possible alternative. The process model emphasises quality of 'input' rather than measuring 'output'. See Stenhouse, 1975, chapter 7, for full discussion.

11 See, for example, John Elliott's various publications arising out of the Ford Teaching Project (Elliott, *et al.*, 1975).

12 Another useful text is Hamilton *et al.* (1977) which traces the move away from Model 1 to the various versions of Model 6. See also Helen Simons (1980).

13 For a number of years there have been proposals to replace GCE (top 20 per cent) and CSE (the next 40 per cent) by a common examination at 16+. Detailed proposals have been drawn up by the Schools Council but the Conservative Government, in 1981–2, was still reluctant to take this step. One problem which would remain would be the 40 per cent of the age-group 'unexamined'. A more radical proposal would be to abolish public examinations at 16+ and replace them by school-based profile assessment.

14 'Diffusion' is defined as a process which happens 'automatically' without organisation, whereas 'dissemination' is the conscious attempt to spread good ideas and so on.

15 The centre-periphery model is based on the idea of innovation or reform directed from a central agency (DES or Schools Council) and then fed out to the periphery (that is, teachers in schools). This is certainly too simple, but to concentrate entirely on periphery development might be equally mistaken. There are links between the centre-periphery model of dissemination and the Research and Development (R and D) model of evaluation – its full title is Research, Development and Dissemination.

8 The Politics of the Curriculum

The strength and weakness of a public curriculum which is shrouded in mystery and changed by stealth has been most obvious in relation to the English primary school.

Tony Becher and Stuart Maclure*

In chapter 7, we saw that evaluation and accountability were frequently said to be 'political' activities. But what does this mean? Is all discussion about curriculum essentially political?

The first point that needs to be made is 'that 'political' in this context does not necessarily have anything to do with political parties (although parties are likely to have differing views on the curriculum which will be related to other political attitudes). 'Political' in this chapter, and elsewhere in the book, is concerned with questions of curriculum control. Behind the apparently simple question 'Who controls the curriculum?' there are at least two controversial issues: the distribution of knowledge in society, and the decision-making processes involved in that distribution. If curriculum is defined as a 'selection from culture' then one important issue is concerned with who decides on the selection and why.

This would appear to suggest that there are three kinds of area which need exploration: first, the pattern of control and influence over the curriculum in any society (that is, who decides on curriculum content and how these decisions are constrained and limited); second, the relation between these decisions and the distribution of 'curriculum chances' (that is access to certain kinds of knowledge via the school system[1]); and finally, how both the decision-making processes and the 'curriculum chances' are related to the different kinds of educational and political ideologies which were discussed in chapter 1.

---

* (1978) *The Politics of Curriculum Change*.

It may help if we immediately attempt to clarify the question of control of the curriculum in one important respect. Popular discussions about curriculum control often seem to assume that control is unitary and total – that is, either teachers should decide on everything about the curriculum, or there must be a centrally controlled uniform curriculum operating in all schools. Reality is, fortunately, much more complicated. In any national system of education there are four or five levels of responsibility:

1 national (in England, the DES);
2 regional (LEAs);
3 institutional (the whole school);
4 departmental (probably only in secondary schools and larger primary schools);
5 individual (the teacher in the classroom).

One interesting aspect of *curriculum* control, however, is that it should not be assumed that control or influence at the national level rests entirely with the DES: this is disputed territory. As we shall see, the 1944 Education Act was more than a little ambiguous on this point, and efforts by the central authority (the Ministry and later the DES) have met with some opposition from LEAs and teachers.[2]

At this point there is another interesting link between control and accountability. In my book on *The Politics of the School Curriculum* (1980) I argued that there had been a significant shift of dominant metaphor: after 1944 and throughout the 1950s, the dominant political metaphor in education was 'partnership' – the idea that the central authority, LEAs, and the teachers, were all partners in the educational enterprise; by 1980, there was much less talk of partnership, but a good deal more of accountability. More of that later. At this stage suffice to say that when one of the partners (the senior partner?) appeared to become too dominating (for example, in 1960, when the Curriculum Study Group was proposed and initiated), the other two partners tended to combine forces and compel the central authority to back down into a less threatening position.

This dislike of central control – especially over the curriculum – has existed for a number of reasons. The first is historical: the beginning of the system of state finance for elementary schools came at a time (1833) of deep distrust of government interference in areas of private life. One fear was that the government might use schools for its own political ends. When the central authority did interfere – in 1862 with the Revised Code and 'payment by results' – it was deeply resented by teachers and others concerned, including HMIs. The second reason for dislike of central control is professional: teachers argue that the curriculum is above all a professional matter not to be tampered with by DES officials who are amateurs in the field. This argument might have been countered had HMI ever become fully incorporated into the central authority, but they have not, and they still retain an institutional independence from the DES, which weakens the claim of central government to press the question of central control too far.

So the argument against central control of the curriculum is essentially that politicians have no right to decide on curriculum matters since they might misuse their powers; and civil servants should be kept away from the curriculum because they lack professional expertise. In *The Politics of the School Curriculum* (1980), I suggested that a more neutral national curriculum body was required – hence the existence of the Schools Council.[3]

I would suggest that in England and Wales, in the early post-1944 period, there was no public controversy over the content of the curriculum and therefore no dispute about control. By the mid-1970s, however, it became clear that political arguments about comprehensive schools were not only organisational issues, but also conflicts about the curriculum; at that stage, the question of curriculum control became a real controversy. As we saw in chapter 7, by the 1970s 'professional' control of the curriculum was increasingly being challenged by parents, governors and employers as well as national politicians. It is, of course, possible to explain the curriculum debate in terms of public disenchantment with educational 'results' (that is, it appeared to some that a lot of money was being spent on education with rather poor value returns). In addition, there was the fear that in some cases, for example the William Tyndale scandal, there appeared to be no way of controlling wayward or incompetent teachers. But it would be wrong to ignore the growth of the *ideological* conflict within education which became particularly concerned with curriculum issues. Whereas in the 1950s and early 1960s it was taken for granted that schools were 'a good thing'; by the late 1960s a serious conflict was already developing. This was symbolised, rather than initiated, by the Black Papers which in this respect should be regarded as important historical documents. The first Black Paper was published in 1969; it was significant because it not only questioned the efficiency of new teaching methods and various curriculum innovations, but also challenged what was seen as a shift in the purpose of schools – that is the argument became one of ideology as well as a question of value for money.

In terms of the ideological discussions in chapter 1, the writers of the Black Papers were classical humanists who complained bitterly about child-centred and progressive education, as well as the kind of 'social engineering' or reconstructionist experiments in comprehensive schools. The debate was confused by the use, on both sides, of highly emotional language, but it was clear that the Black Paper writers felt that education should be concerned with transmitting our cultural heritage to a minority of able pupils (preferably in well established public and grammar schools) by means of a curriculum based on traditional subjects, whereas the majority of pupils should be prepared for the world of work in separate secondary schools. Their attack was, therefore, a mixture of classical humanism and a kind of utilitarian philosophy.

In many respects, the counter-attack was extremely confused. Progressive means (teaching methods) were confused with reconstructionist ends. Egalitarians wanted comprehensive schools so that young people could have a better education, but because the purpose of that education was often ill-defined, the debate became centred on how to teach rather than what children should be expected to learn – the focus of the conflict was more likely to be 'progressive', child-centred teaching methods, rather than the real question of curriculum content.[4] It was for this reason that any evidence about teaching methods (for example, Neville Bennett's research) was seized upon as evidence in favour of a traditional curriculum and a way of criticising, for example, mixed ability teaching in comprehensive schools.

The question of standards was also related to ideology. Any evidence obtained from tests of reading scores or mathematical ability were used to call into question progressive primary schools as well as the continued existence of comprehensive education. At this point it is necessary to link these ideological arguments with political parties, although a number of qualifications will have to be made. The Conservative Party, on the whole, favours an elitist approach to education and advocates a different kind of educational menu for the privileged minority from what should be made available to the majority of pupils. For them, equality of opportunity means a 'ladder of opportunity' for a small minority (including a few of the deserving poor) who can 'benefit from' an academic secondary curriculum or even higher education. On the other hand, although the Labour Party contains many deviants, the essential democratic socialist philosophy of education is represented by the 'broad highway' metaphor – the idea that *all* young people should have a good education (alas, not clearly described or even outlined in any Labour Party documents). There is, of course, a close relationship between wanting to educate all young people and wanting them to be treated humanely in schools – hence the apparent link with child-centred teaching methods. But I would suggest this is sometimes a false trail for social reconstructionists to follow. There is a considerable difference between treating all children humanely or with respect, and letting them do whatever they feel like doing. R. S. Peters has remarked (1966) that it is not always in children's interests to allow them to pursue their interests all the time![5]

Bearing in mind these ideological conflicts, let us now return to the five-level model of curriculum control. The first obvious point to be made is that ideological differences may exist at four of the five levels (and perhaps even at level 5 within the teacher's own mind!). At level 1, for example, there may well be differences in ideology between the politicians themselves, between DES officials and perhaps between DES officials and HMIs. At level 2 similar differences may exist between local politicians and the permanent officers. At level 3, there may be ideological differences between teachers in the same school. This is all part of sorting out an educational policy within a pluralistic society. More public political conflict is likely to occur, however, when the dominant ideology at one level is directly opposed to the dominant ideology at another level: for example, if a Conservative Party exerts pressure on the DES to impose a curriculum which is in conflict with the vast majority of teachers or their representatives in the form of the NUT. Our model would then become much more complex.

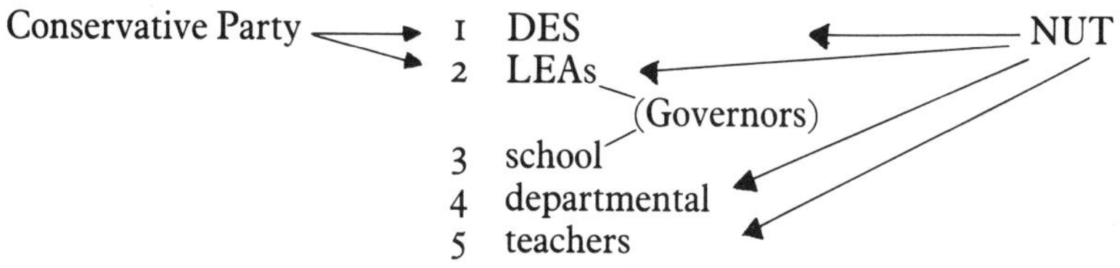

Figure 6

In a democratic society, I suggest it would be undesirable for all the curriculum control to be concentrated at any one level – whether at the centre (level 1) or for schools (level 3) to have complete freedom to decide on a curriculum. I have given an example (page 118) of a conflict (which became a real issue in 1979 over the publication by the DES of *Framework for the School Curriculum* which was eventually modified in 1981). There could be many other such conflicts – for example, between an LEA wanting to ban political education or sex education and a school which regarded them as of central importance. Such conflicts may be regarded as productive tensions within a pluralist system. Part of the function of the cultural analysis approach to curriculum planning will be to provide guidance at the national level on the parameters and limits of negotiation; in the political education example above, it would *not* simply be a matter of reaching a compromise, but of pointing out that some kind of political education is, from a cultural analysis point of view, essential, and that the debate should be limited to what kind of political education might be appropriate in a particular school. For this reason, a set of national guidelines might actually protect teachers from too much local interference!

Conflict is inevitable, but much of the conflict about curriculum control would be clarified, though not completely eliminated, if the curricular responsibilities of each of the five levels could be defined a little more closely, though never conclusively. It would seem to me to be reasonable, for example, to say that at level 5 the teacher in the classroom is free to decide (within the limits of professionalism) what to teach in particular lessons, and what methods would be most appropriate for a particular class. This is an aspect of professional autonomy. But it does not give the teacher *complete* freedom to do anything he or she likes in the classroom and call it education. The teacher must be constrained by syllabuses agreed with colleagues (level 4) and by agreement within the school about the whole curriculum (level 3) as well as certain professional standards agreed nationally. The head teacher also has responsibility to the LEA. None of this would be necessarily opposed to the idea of establishing nationally agreed guidelines on the school curriculum, so long as they were not detailed and not imposed on a reluctant teaching profession by nonprofessional civil servants at the DES. The model would then appear as follows:

Level 1 (national)
Guidelines by Schools Council or other appropriate body.
Level 2 (regional) (LEA)
National guidelines co-ordinated and implemented.
Level 3 (institutional) (the school)
The whole curriculum worked out by the academic board of the school (or other committee structure)[6] reporting to governors and indirectly responsible to LEA.
Level 4 (departmental)
Syllabuses agreed by all teachers in departments.
Level 5 (individual)
The classroom teacher free to decide on lessons and appropriate methods.

This brings us to another necessary dimension which needs to be added to the model. Not only is it important in any debate about

Table 11

level \ aspect	curriculum	pedagogy	evaluation
1 national			
2 regional			
3 institutional			
4 departmental			
5 individual			

curriculum control to be specific about the level of control under discussion, it is also necessary on some occasions to be specific as to the aspect of curriculum being referred to it. Bernstein (1975), for example, has made a useful distinction between curriculum content, pedagogy (teacher/pupil relations and teaching methods) and curriculum evaluation (including examinations, assessment and testing). Given the five levels of curriculum control and three aspects of curriculum at each level, we now have a matrix with 15 cells or spaces, see table 11.

This 15 cell matrix may be used either to compare different societies at any one time, or to trace changes within a given society over a period of time.

In a completely totalitarian regime, for example, the theory might be that all three aspects, curriculum, pedagogy and evaluation, are centrally controlled and determined at level 1. In such a society the model would be indicated as follows:

Table 12

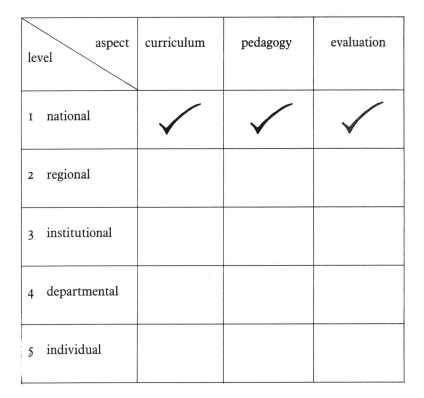

level \ aspect	curriculum	pedagogy	evaluation
1 national	✓	✓	✓
2 regional			
3 institutional			
4 departmental			
5 individual			

In practice, however, it is never possible to control pedagogy (even with an inspector sitting in every classroom). A more likely model in a centralised but probably non-totalitarian system would be for the curriculum to be prescribed nationally, the pedagogy to be largely in the discretion of the classroom teacher and the evaluation to be a school responsibility, but perhaps moderated regionally. In that case, the model would be as follows:

Table 13

aspect / level	curriculum	pedagogy	evaluation
1 national	✓		
2 regional			✓
3 institutional			✓
4 departmental			
5 individual		✓	

This would, of course, be an over-simplification of reality. In practice any national curriculum will be modified regionally and within the school as well as by individual teachers; the model only attempts to show the overall pattern of control in a necessarily simplified way.

Now for an example about changes over time. In England, since the 1944 Education Act, there have been interesting changes in control. I have already said that the wording of the 1944 Act was unclear as regards curriculum control, but in practice after 1944 there was little attempt to establish any national curriculum (apart from the Religious Education requirement which was clearly specified). Post-war Ministers of Education apparently went out of their way to re-assure LEAs and the teaching profession generally that they had no wish to influence curriculum.[7] LEAs, in turn, passed on the responsibility for curriculum to school governors (or managers in primary schools) who tended to regard this as a professional matter for the head teacher and his (her) assistant to organise.

Two further points need to be made about the immediate post-1944 educational context. First, most LEAs developed tripartite secondary systems,[8] with a selection system of some kind at age 11 (the 11+ test); this tended to act as a powerful constraint on the primary school curriculum with a built-in measuring device in terms of the success rate of pupils 'passing' the 11+ examination. The second point that has to be made about the post-1944 situation is that secondary grammar schools were even more constrained by the school leaving examination at 16 (then called the School Certificate). Ministers of Education could, therefore, afford to be reasonably relaxed about the content of the curriculum since there were such powerful evaluation controls which, to some extent, exerted a constraining influence on both content and standards. Thus the control pattern in 1945 for secondary and primary schools in England would have looked something like table 14.

During the 1950s, two important developments took place. The first was that in 1951 the old School Certificate, which had been a group examination[9] was replaced by the single subject General Certificate of Education examination (GCE 'O' level). At a stroke, one important aspect of curriculum planning, that is what subjects all pupils should be required to take, became a school responsibility rather than an external pattern imposed by an examining board.[10] This tendency for the school to have great discretion over individual pupils' choice of subject was extended still further when another examination – the Certificate of Secondary Education (CSE) – was introduced, also on a single subject basis, in 1964.[11]

The second major shift in control relationships was caused by the gradual loss of confidence in 11+ testing throughout the 1950s, and the consequent move by more and more LEAs away from segregated secondary systems; comprehensive schools became more common, and after 1966 became official policy. In

Table 14

level \ aspect	curriculum	pedagogy	evaluation
1 national	✓		
2 regional			✓
3 institutional	✓		✓
4 departmental			
5 individual		✓	

some LEAs the dreaded 11+ testing was completely abolished; in others it was retained but became much less important in determining individual pupils' destinies. For primary schools generally it meant that a constraint was removed, and some primary schools may have rejoiced in this freedom to spend more time on 'creative' work and less on the kind of basic attainments which had been demanded by the 11+ tests in English, arithmetic and 'verbal reasoning'. Hard data on this tends to be difficult to come by, but there probably was a shift in emphasis in some primary schools, although there is no evidence to support the view that this resulted in a serious drop in standards. More importantly from the point of view of curriculum control, our model for primary and secondary schools would now be changed to the following:

Table 15

level \ aspect	curriculum	pedagogy	evaluation
1 national			
2 regional			
3 institutional	✓		✓
4 departmental			
5 individual		✓	

The significance of this new pattern is clear: there was now very little curriculum control at levels 1 and 2 – nationally and regionally. There could be influence, of course, by means of circulars and other documents and by visits from inspectors. But the degree of responsibility possessed by schools themselves was now considerably increased. It should also be pointed out that at precisely this time, the 1950s and 1960s, there was an acute shortage of teachers in the UK. The number of students in training colleges increased from 31,000 in 1959–60 to 54,000 in 1963–4 and to a target of 80,000 by 1971. Without accepting the doctrine that 'more means worse' there is some evidence to suggest that the quality of the weakest entries into the profession during those years was almost certainly not as high as it should have been.

By the 1960s, it has been suggested by Kogan (1978) and others that the tide was beginning to turn and that there was a certain loss of confidence in schools in their ability to satisfy the very high expectations. By 1969, the Black Papers began to appear, criticising not only the lack of efficiency in schools, but also the dangerous ideological viewpoints possessed by many teachers. In 1960, there had been an attempt by a Conservative Minister of Education, Sir David Eccles, to increase central influence but probably not central control. Manzer (1970) claims that the first suggestion of a venture by the central authority into 'the secret garden of the curriculum' came during a debate in the House of Commons on the Crowther Report (21 March 1960). Eccles expressed his regret that education debates were devoted so much to bricks and mortar and organisation, and stated that he would try to make the Ministry's voice heard rather more often and positively and, no doubt, more controversially on what was taught in schools. Manzer also claims that it was because of divided opinion in the Inspectorate that it took two years before the Curriculum Study Group (CSG) was officially announced. When it came in 1962 the announcement was made without prior consultation with organised educational interests. Predictably, the NUT and the LEAs objected strongly to what was seen as a bid for central direction of the curriculum. This fear was not allayed by Sir David Eccles talking about the CSG as a relatively small 'commando-like unit' which would make raids into the curriculum.

Perhaps more significant of real political change than the rather clumsy public utterances of the Minister was a statement included in a letter by the Permanent Secretary of the Ministry of Education to the educational associations. This described the CSG as a response to the pressure of rapid change and increases in knowledge which justified the involvement of the Ministry and the Inspectorate in this field of curriculum development. It is probably true that it was not the case that the CSG was intended to be a general takeover bid for the control of the curriculum.[12]

Nevertheless, it was seen as a threat by teachers and LEAs; an alliance of Sir William Alexander, representing the LEAs, and Sir Ronald Gould, of the NUT, demanded that the CSG be replaced by a *representative* body. In the short run, they won the battle but I suspect that in the longer run teachers lost the war. In May 1963 the next Minister, Sir Edward Boyle, announced that a Schools Council would be formed thus providing the representative body asked for by Gould and Alexander. A committee was set up under the chairmanship of Sir John Lockwood which reported in March 1964. The Schools Council would be organised as a free association of partners, not advisory to the Ministry of Education alone, but to all interests. An important aspect of the constitution was that teachers would be guaranteed a majority on most of the important Council committees.

The Schools Council was born and might have had enormous influence. I believe, however, that an important opportunity was lost at this stage. It could have been possible for the Schools Council to have become the 'level 1', the national body for establishing national curriculum guidelines. It possessed real independence from party political control as well as from the DES, and the opportunity was there for the Schools Council to become an independent authority nationally. Unfortunately, the Council took a different route: the anti-centralist doctrine that schools alone must be responsible for curriculum planning was espoused. Instead of looking at the whole curriculum, the Schools Council embarked upon an expensive programme of curriculum development projects on what can only be called a cafeteria basis: teachers would be offered three or four different kinds of science, but no one seemed prepared to say that all children should have a right of access to certain kinds of knowledge including science. This doctrine was perhaps a combination of a genuine dislike of too much central control, plus an over-optimistic view of what the average school could achieve without guidance (or possibly an underestimation of the difficulties involved in curriculum planning, curriculum innovation and, above all, the problem of disseminating good ideas from the centre (Schools Council) to the periphery – the schools).

Much of the curriculum development work of the Schools Council was of very high standard. Later criticisms of the Council's work as being mediocre were grossly unfair. But it was not until 1975[13] that a document appeared from the Council on the whole curriculum, and it was so enfeebled by successive redrafting that it had very little impact on schools and was never accepted as a Schools Council policy document. Only in 1981 did a firm statement on the whole curriculum appear with the Schools Council imprimatur – *The Practical Curriculum* – and by that time it was too late. The DES takeover bid was by now well under way. But that is to anticipate another important development (see below).

The 1962–4 bid for central influence, if it existed at all, was defeated by a combination of teachers and LEAs. The probability is that civil servants as well as HMI were divided on the degree of central influence on the curriculum which they felt desirable. This appears to be the view of Manzer as well as Kogan. But by the end of the 1970s there were many more voices being raised in favour of greater central influence, some of which were discussed in chapter 7 in the context of accountability (see pages 91–6). In addition there is some evidence that ministers and civil servants were increasingly embarrassed by their lack of knowledge about what schools were doing in terms of curriculum and this was directly connected with the lack of any central policy on the curriculum. It has also been suggested, but hard evidence is difficult to produce, that civil servants at the DES were looked down upon by their colleagues in more centralist departments for the DES's lack of power in the curriculum arena which was becoming more and more controversial. The closest to a public declaration of this view came in 1975–6 when the DES was scrutinised by the House of Commons Expenditure Committee. In their study of policy-making in the DES, the Education Sub-Committee made two complaints about the Department: first, that the DES was excessively secretive, and second that it lacked an adequate planning organisation. If there was any doubt about the DES liking for secrecy, evidence was not long in coming because the DES officials promptly refused to make available to the Committee itself the planning and analysis review papers on which educational policies had been based! Although at the time the DES appeared to shrug off the two main criticisms, it is more than likely that note was taken about the lack of policy within the DES and that a firmer line would be taken in future years.

In 1976, there was also a report by an external body – the OECD[14] – on the DES. The OECD also criticised the DES's secrecy as well as the lack of clear planning.

By 1976, pressures were certainly building up for the DES to take a more active role in educational planning including a greater degree of influence over the curriculum. During the previous year (1975) the Secretary of State for Education, Fred Mulley, was asked by the Prime Minister, James Callaghan, to produce a report on standards in schools. The result was a secret Yellow Book which was, perhaps deliberately, leaked to the Press in 1976, a little while before the Prime Minister's October speech at Ruskin College. The Yellow Book was critical of the 'child-centred' approach to primary school teaching and cast some doubt on standards. The curriculum of secondary schools was also mentioned, and some bald and atheoretical points made about the inclusion of certain subjects such as modern languages in the curriculum. The Prime Minister's Ruskin Speech, however, was watered down to some extent and the main message was about education in a changing industrial society. It was in that respect unbalanced since it over-emphasised the function of education which is concerned with servicing manpower needs, but neglected more important areas.

The Speech was not regarded as particularly controversial and led to the so-called Great Debate in Education. Throughout 1977 there were a number of regional conferences discussing the primary curriculum as well as the secondary curriculum, the assessment of standards, the training of teachers and, inevitably, school and working life. This served as background to the Green Paper *Education in Schools: A Consultative Document* (July 1977) which referred back to the Ruskin Speech and continued to emphasise the connection between school and the adult world of work. Comments were made directly on the curriculum, arguing, for example, that too little attention was paid to the basic skills of reading, writing and arithmetic. Above all, reference was made to the fundamental need for Britain to survive economically in a highly competitive world through the efficiency of its industry and commerce. More importantly, the Green Paper served to announce a change in emphasis by the DES. There was to be a new positive approach on policy including the curriculum. Secretaries of State should not abdicate their responsibilities in this field and they would seek to establish a broad agreement with 'their partners in the education service' on a framework for the curriculum. This 'broad agreement' would include a policy on whether there should be a core or protected part of the curriculum.

Finally, it was announced that LEAs would be asked by means of a circular to carry out a review, in their own areas, of curriculum arrangements and report the results to the DES within about a year. In due course the DES Circular 14/77 *LEA Arrangements for the School Curriculum* was issued and a return requested. The circular was not simply a request for information, but included subtle policy directives: for example, there was a strong push in the direction of a common curriculum and a special section on modern languages.

When these returns from the LEAs were received by the DES and analysed, a report was published (1979) which was critical of the LEAs in two respects. First, the DES complained that some LEAs seemed not to possess adequate information about the curriculum in their schools; secondly, they complained that many

LEAs appeared to lack a clear policy on curriculum. The next stage would be to require LEAs to put this right. In December 1979, the DES published its *Framework for the School Curriculum* which was a very unsatisfactory document, much criticised by teachers, some LEAs and other educationists. It was confused and over-prescriptive, even suggesting that schools should devote 10 per cent of their timetable to mathematics, 10 per cent to English and so on. Once again, no theoretical justification was given for any of these recommendations.

As a result of these criticisms and other kinds of consultation, in 1981 a revised version was published by the DES with the title of *The School Curriculum*. It was regarded as a better document, largely because it left out the percentages which were so offensive in *Framework*, but in other respects it was equally unsatisfactory. By emphasising certain 'basic' subjects, other areas of the curriculum were automatically devalued. The result was a policy document on curriculum which emphasised English, mathematics, science and modern languages at precisely the time when, owing to the problem of falling rolls in schools, there was in any case a tendency to 'cut out the frills' such as music. Once again, LEAs were warned that they would be asked for further information about the implementation of curriculum policy within a reasonable period. In other words, *The School Curriculum* was not simply a discussion document, but was in some respects a kind of minimum curriculum policy. I will resist the temptation to review the whole document critically at this stage, since my particular interest is, in this chapter, simply to illustrate the tendency of the DES to take a much stronger line on curriculum policy.

Another point needs to be made at this stage. Since 1975 another pressure on the curriculum had been emerging: the Assessment of Performance Unit (APU). There is much confusion about whether the APU was originally intended to serve the needs of disadvantaged children, especially immigrant children, or whether it was a proposal to monitor standards nationally. One suspicion is that it had long been planned as a monitoring standards exercise, but the DES seized the opportunity of a parliamentary debate on educational disadvantage in 1974 to announce the Unit, giving it a different emphasis. Certainly as the years passed by there was more and more discussion of monitoring standards and less concern with disadvantaged children. Although officially the APU line has been that it has nothing to do with curriculum planning, and APU officers have repeatedly emphasised that they did not wish to influence the curriculum, it is highly likely that any set of tests even if used on a light sampling basis[15] will have a backwash effect on the school curriculum. There is almost inevitably a tendency for teachers to look at this year's tests and modify their teaching for next year, to some extent.

The APU has also been subject to a number of methodological criticisms about sampling and the particular model being used, but a discussion of its procedures would be out of place here.[16] It will be enough to say that the probability is that any unit of this kind within the DES is likely to have some influence on what is being taught in school. This may now be an unfortunate influence because the original model which would have been a 'cross curriculum model'[17] has apparently been abandoned and the only tests that are likely to be used in schools will be English, mathematics and science. Once again, this is likely to have a damaging effect on schools' curricula because it will emphasise certain subjects and, therefore, inevitably channel resources in one direction rather than another.

In terms of the model we have used throughout this chapter, it would now appear that 'the centre' has gained more national influence over both curriculum and evaluation, leaving only pedagogy in the hands of teachers themselves. See table 16 below.

Two further points need to be made at this stage, one by way of qualification and the other providing additional evidence of the swing of power to the centre. The first is that it would not be correct to assume that there is some kind of monolithic control of the curriculum at national level by DES. Over the last five years or so there have been increasing signs that HMIs are not entirely in agreement with DES policy on the curriculum.[18] It is significant that at the same time as the 1979 *Framework* document appeared, there was also published an HMI *View of the Curriculum* which represented a much broader and richer approach to the curriculum – owing something to the cultural analysis tradition. *A View of the Curriculum* followed an even better HMI document, *Curriculum 11–16*, which had set out the idea of a common curriculum based not on subjects, but on eight 'areas of experience'. Although there is nothing directly contradictory between, say, *Curriculum 11–16* and *The School Curriculum*, a different approach had been used. Whereas *The School Curriculum* is subject based and views the curriculum in a rather narrow way, *Curriculum 11–16* and other HMI documents including *Aspects of Secondary Education* show a concern for the whole development of pupils throughout

Table 16

aspect / level	curriculum	pedagogy	evaluation
1 national	✓		✓
2 regional			
3 institutional			
4 departmental			
5 individual		✓	

their period of compulsory schooling. It would, therefore, be open to schools to take more notice of the HMI model than the guidelines published by the DES. It is to be hoped that they will do this.

My second point concerns further evidence about the tendency of the centre to exert more influence on the school curriculum. 1982 was significant for a number of disconnected events. It was announced by the Secretary of State for Education, Sir Keith Joseph, that the Schools Council would be abolished and replaced by two advisory bodies, the members of which would be nominated by the Secretary of State himself. This is important for two reasons. First, it reverses the victory of 1960–2 when a combination of the NUT plus LEAs forced the Minister to change his decision on precisely this issue, that a curriculum advisory body should be representative rather than nominated. The second aspect of the 1982 decision is the strange division to be made between advice on curriculum and advice on examinations, which also runs counter to professional opinion at least since the 1940s. There is a suspicion here that the Schools Council has been seen as too powerful a rival for the DES in the curriculum policy game and is, therefore, to be eliminated and replaced by a more subservient body, appointed rather than representative.

Finally, 1982 was notable for central interference in the curriculum in ways which would in previous years have been unthinkable. In March, Sir Keith Joseph, in a speech to the Institute of Directors, said that he thought that schools should teach the moral virtue of profits. It might be unwise to regard one speech to a specific audience as evidence of a change of policy, but Sir Keith Joseph was the Secretary of State for Education and it would not be unreasonable to regard any public statement as something he would wish to press on schools. Perhaps it would be safer simply to see this as an indication that for schools to preach the moral virtue of free enterprise and the pursuit of profit might be regarded by some politicians as non-political, whereas suggesting that schools should encourage children to see the virtue of nationalised industries would be regarded as highly political.

Later in the same year (May 1982) another example of government interference in the curriculum was noted. A pamphlet *The Balanced View* was prepared by the Central Office of Information as part of a government counter-campaign against growing support for disarmament including nuclear disarmament. Apparently ministers were worried by the growth of the Campaign for Nuclear Disarmament (CND) in schools and were anxious to put the other side. The pamphlet dismissed the unilateral position as a neglect of defence and drew a parallel with the follies of the 1930s. Once again, this example might be seen as direct interference by government in school curriculum. What is perhaps even more surprising was the comparative lack of controversy raised by such an apparently provocative document.

Perhaps this marks acquiescence by the teaching profession to the fact of more central influence over the curriculum. If that is the case, then the teaching profession certainly ought to bear in mind the implications of the model I have used in this chapter and attempt to redress the balance. In other words, if there is a swing to the centre in terms of control of the content of the curriculum, then it would be perfectly reasonable for teachers to demand more involvement in curriculum evaluation. There are many good arguments in favour of 16+ evaluation being in the hands of the schools themselves, perhaps with some regional moderation being carried out by the existing examining boards. The 16+ examinations have many faults and are extremely costly to operate. Whereas in the past it would have been unreasonable for teachers to have expected to control the curriculum content, pedagogy and evaluation, now it would appear quite reasonable for teachers to have a greater involvement in end-of-school assessment and certification since they have yielded so much of their control over the whole curriculum to central authority and LEAs.

Summary

This brief outline of the changing pattern of control of the curriculum in England should serve to illustrate three points. First, that when we talk of curriculum control, it is important to be clear about the five levels where control may be in dispute. Second, that arguments about control may be related to professional concern or to ideological differences – or both. Finally, that disputes about control are rarely simple and straightforward – there are likely to be mixed motives and disputes within disputes. To some extent such tensions may be productive, but it may also be that for them to become productive the real issues have to be made more open – and there is at least a suspicion that bureaucracies, such as the DES, prefer manipulation and subterfuge to genuine debate.

NOTES

1   Sociologists have collected much demographic data which shows that, for example, there are significant differences between social classes on the 'chances' of suffering from certain diseases, getting certain kinds of jobs and so on – these are referred to as 'life chances'; sociologists of education have attempted to show the relation between 'life chances' and educational opportunity or 'educational chances'. I am suggesting a further division of the latter category – curriculum chances – which would be concerned with educational access, not to institutions, but to knowledge.

2   See Becher and Maclure (1978), chapter 4, for an interesting discussion of this topic.

3   I suggested (1980) that if the Schools Council did not exist, it would be necessary to invent it. I do not think that Sir Keith Joseph's 1982 proposal to abolish the Schools Council proves me wrong, since his proposal includes the suggestion that the Council should be replaced by a small curriculum advisory body – the members of which would be nominated by the Secretary of State.

4   It appears to be the case that many 'progressive' schools have given little attention to the content of the curriculum. This may be deliberate in the case of those who believe, as part of the child-centred ideology, that children should choose for themselves; or it may be accidental in the sense that 'progressive' teachers tend to concentrate on 'the children' and their happiness rather than the curriculum. Reconstructionists, however, in their search for social change, need to change the curriculum and use it positively. They have sometimes been side-tracked into demolishing the traditional curriculum without having an adequately planned replacement.

5   A useful summary of that debate can be found in R. S. Peters (1968).

6   See chapter 6 for a discussion of possible committee structure.

7   George Tomlinson, for example, became famous for stating that 'Minister knows nowt about curriculum'.

8   Secondary grammar for the academically minded, secondary technical for those who had technical abilities and secondary modern for the rest. In fact very few secondary technical schools ever existed and most tended to fade away leaving a bi-partite system rather than a tri-partite (roughly 20 per cent grammar, 80 per cent modern, although the local variation in that proportion was enormous).

9   To be awarded a School Certificate a candidate had to pass at least five subjects, including certain compulsory subjects. It is referred to as a 'group examination' in contrast to 'single subject examinations' where a certificate is awarded for one subject or any combination of subjects.

10 The School Certificate was a group examination, the rules of which had been gradually relaxed, but these requirements were supplemented by the regulations for matriculation which stipulated certain subjects such as English, mathematics and science. It was the matriculation requirements rather than the School Certificate itself which imposed a kind of common core curriculum.

11 Whereas GCE was intended for roughly the top 20 per cent of the ability rate, the CSE covered the next 40 per cent thus leaving another 40 per cent unexaminable group at the bottom. Edmund Leach once complained about a university system where no fewer than 90 per cent of participants were predestined to be labelled second rate or worse, and asked 'Could anything be more absurd?' I would suggest that a system whereby 40 per cent of the school population are

regarded as total failures is even more absurd.

12   See Maurice Kogan (1978) whose evidence must be particularly valuable since he was at that time a civil servant at the DES and worked within the CSG.

13   Schools Council Working Paper 53, *The Whole Curriculum 13–16* (1975). In the same year a much better document also appeared for the 8–13 age group, *The Curriculum in the Middle Years* (Working Paper 55). But little use was ever made of this by the Schools Council: they always appeared to be apologetic about any document which discussed the whole curriculum in terms of what all schools should be doing!

14   The Organisation for Economic Co-operation and Development (OECD) was founded in 1961 to stimulate economic progress and world trade. Part of its function is to review education systems and to make recommendations to its member countries.

15   Part of the policy of the APU – and one of its 'selling points' to teachers – was that there would be no 'blanket-testing' (that is, every child in a class or in a school) but only 'light sampling' (about one child in 200). Thus, it was hoped, disruption of teaching would be minimised and 'backwash' effects (teaching to the test) would *not* occur.

16   See Lawton (1980) for a fuller discussion of the APU or Lacey and Lawton (1981).

17   Brian Kay (1975) originally proposed a model based on six lines of development:

   verbal;
   mathematical;
   scientific;
   ethical;
   aesthetic;
   physical.

Unfortunately it looks as though testing will be focused on the first three of these areas.

18   It may be equally simplistic to assume that all the DES officials have a single view, or that all HMI are united on curriculum content and control. We must await an internal study of DES and HMI.

9 Curriculum Planning in a Plural Society

> The weight of . . . evidence would appear to support the case that egalitarian reforms have failed. But such a view is premissed on the assumption that egalitarian concerns have, in fact, been consistently pursued by post-war governments. This seems more doubtful.
>
> John Gray*

Throughout this book I have been arguing that a major reform of the English educational system would involve the development of a common curriculum. The main argument in support of that view has been that if common, comprehensive schools are to be credible, they must transmit a common culture by means of a common curriculum. The task of curriculum planning then becomes a process of cultural analysis – selecting the most worthwhile and relevant aspects of our common culture so that access to important kinds of knowledge and areas of experience can be made available to *all* pupils. I have attempted to outline the basis for determining both the common culture and a common curriculum, as well as commenting upon other proposals such as the HMI discussion document *Curriculum 11–16*.

A number of objections have been raised to my proposals for a common culture curriculum, two of which will be examined in this chapter. The first objection is concerned with the view that a common curriculum would be undesirable for working-class children since the curriculum would inevitably be constructed in such a way as to provide a built-in advantage for children from the upper and middle classes and would fail to reflect working-class culture. The second objection involves the argument that in a multi-ethnic, multicultural society there is no common culture and, therefore, a common curriculum would be impossible or, if attempted, inappropriate. I will deal with each of these objections in turn.

---

* (1981) In SIMON, B. and TAYLOR, W. *Education in the Eighties*.

1   A Working-Class Curriculum

The major objection to a common curriculum from this point of view is that a curriculum will necessarily be dominated by middle-class values and prejudices, and that the only effective way of counter-attacking the built-in educational injustices within English society would be to construct a specifically working-class curriculum.

Undoubtedly, it is the case that the schooling system, as it now exists, appears to favour middle-class pupils. Many, but not all, working-class pupils 'under-achieve' despite various attempts that have been made to encourage equality of opportunity in education over the last forty years. Before 1944, it was assumed that simply providing all children with free access to secondary schools would solve the problem of unequal chances. Unfortunately, although the 1944 Education Act made secondary education both free and compulsory, most LEAs provided different kinds of schools to cater for supposedly different kinds of ability. It was soon discovered (Glass, 1954) that there was a very high correlation between measured ability and class, so that middle-class children were generally over-represented in secondary grammar schools and working-class children were tending to be selected for secondary modern schools. There were two possible explanations for this unequal representation: either that working-class children were, on the whole, less able; or that the selection system somehow discriminated against working-class pupils. Sociologists during the 1950s (for example, Floud *et al.*, 1956) discussed the various possible explanations for working-class under-achievement at 11+, including the linguistic disadvantages of working-class pupils in the test situations which demanded high levels of verbal skills. Such research findings provided further arguments for the establishment of non-selective comprehensive schools as well as the abolition of testing at 11+.

When comprehensive schools were established it was soon found (Ford, 1968) that working-class children still tended to be under-achievers and to be over-represented in the lower streams of comprehensive schools. This kind of evidence encouraged those egalitarian reformers who disliked streaming to press for mixed ability groups which would avoid conscious or unconscious discrimination against working-class pupils. But still they tend to under-achieve even in those situations. Why? One theory which attempted to deal with this problem was the view that the problem existed within the curriculum itself. The curriculum it was argued was 'socially constructed' in such a way as to handicap those who were already less privileged within society.

The 'curriculum as a social construct' theory takes many forms, some of them more extreme than others. What many have in common is the assertion that knowledge has developed partly as a form of social control: those who possess certain kinds of knowledge endow it with an arbitrary status and importance. Certain kinds of knowledge have become a badge of rank to identify an elite and to exclude the outsiders. Latin and Greek in the nineteenth century public school curriculum were obvious examples – they marked out those who had a 'good', that is classical, education; less obvious examples might include the fact that some aspects of so-called middle-class culture are highly valued (opera, for example) whereas working-class culture (for example, pop music) is not valued socially or educationally. M. F. D. Young (1971) rightly rebuked sociologists for 'taking' working-class failure in education as a problem rather than 'making' their own problem by questioning the validity of the curriculum by which working-class children were judged. Young used and developed Marx's assertion that education in a capitalist society was a tool of the ruling-class interest: why assume that education is 'good' or 'worthwhile' in itself?

Unfortunately, in my view, Young went too far in suggesting that all knowledge was arbitrary and even that rationality itself was a mere social convention. In attempting to refute this extreme case I suggested (1975) that it was misleading to assume that because some knowledge is socially constructed, *all* knowledge divisions are arbitrary and *all* values simply a matter of taste. I would agree with Marx and Mannheim, that some kinds of knowledge – including mathematics and science – are class-less. A class-free common curriculum should be based on knowledge and experience which could be justified by criteria other than middle-class preference, that is, by a process of cultural analysis. It is clearly no part of my intention to prop up an unjust social system by manipulating the educational system to maintain inequalities; nor do I believe that a properly planned common curriculum could possibly have that effect.

In 1979 I was, however, taken to task in an interesting essay by Uldis Ozolins, who rightly criticised *Class, Culture and the Curriculum* (1975) for its inadequate analysis of class. Ozolins complains that I dismiss the idea of a working-class curriculum by demonstrating that a working-class life style does not possess enough content of quality to provide an adequate cultural basis for a curriculum. Part of Ozolins' objection is that I rely too much on arguments about working-class life style whereas the most important feature of class is *not* life style, but relational factors – that is, differential access to wealth and power. Ozolins, therefore, suggests that a suitable working-class curriculum would be one which would equip working-class students with the means of challenging that status quo effectively and, presumably, gaining more wealth and power themselves.

   I agree. The relational factor is the more important aspect of class, and any social engineering attempt to use education to promote greater equality should focus on differential access to power and resources rather than on the life style aspects of class in our society. Yet sooner or later we are forced to consider the question of curriculum content, and this is necessarily a problem of cultural analysis. We have to ask what are the most important, worthwhile and relevant aspects of life that we want to make available to the next generation. Ozolins, seeking to increase working-class awareness of justice (as well as providing basic relevant knowledge for real life) recommends the kind of working-class curriculum outlined by Robins and Cohen (1978) in *Knuckle Sandwich*:

1   literacy and communication skills;
2   self-health, social biology and sex education;
3   history of working-class life and struggle – local, national and
    international;
4   studies in applied science and technology.

   A number of interesting points emerge from considering this proposed working-class curriculum. First, why sub-divide the curriculum into four headings? It could be argued that they fall neatly into easily recognised categories: for example, (1) is English; (2) is a selection from biology; (3) is a kind of history; (4) is science and technology. This illustrates a point which I have been trying to make in the face of criticisms from writers like Ozolins that knowledge is not a seamless garment: even in its most radical formulation it falls into categories. Whether these categories are 'God-given' or 'man-made' is almost irrelevant – we appear to need some kind of sub-classification of knowledge in order to know what we are talking about. My common curriculum was an attempt to make as few arbitrary divisions as possible and to earmark those kinds of knowledge and experience that all young people should have access to.

The Robins and Cohen working-class curriculum seems to me to be a little thin, but would fit nicely into my own categories. So why does Ozolins want to call it a working-class curriculum? The answer, it is clear from his own paper, is not so much directed at the content of the curriculum but at the school as an institution. Willis (1977) and others have suggested that schools, *as they are at present organised*, alienate working-class pupils – especially boys. Any programme of educational reform will have to take that problem into consideration as well as the content of the curriculum and, I would suggest, better pupil/teacher relationships. But to offer working-class children something different in content from middle-class children would be to run the risk of selling them short.

If we apply cultural analysis to a whole school setting, then it will become clear that three kinds of reform must proceed side by side: improved *curriculum* content, a complete rethinking of teacher/pupil relationships and teaching methods (pedagogy), and finally the kind of school *organisation* that would make all that possible including improved evaluation. This is not to advocate a *laissez-faire* 'progressive' approach to schooling. Far from it! What is needed is a clear view of the kind of educational experiences all children have a right to, and then to consider the kinds of teaching and school organisation which are essential means to that end. Only in that sense would the curriculum be child-centred. As I indicated in chapter 8, there is a clear need to abolish the present system of secondary schools examinations and the structure that goes along with it whereby nearly half of all secondary pupils are seen as 'failures'. This is a damaging and alienating anti-educational context for the majority of pupils. It is also true that some pupils are alienated by the curricula they are offered in secondary schools. But to think that this complex set of problems can be solved by a simple proletarianisation of the curriculum would be extremely naïve. Gramsci (1971) was surely correct in his suggestion that there is no short cut to power for the working classes – they must somehow acquire a mastery of the relevant knowledge.[1]

It is also important that the aims of education are not seen in terms of social mobility. I have mentioned several times the necessity for the curriculum to serve the need of *all* young people; thus it is important to stress that schooling is not concerned only with those destined for higher education or for a professional career. It is concerned with all young people including – perhaps especially – those who may not succeed in getting any kind of job when they leave school.

This is very much in line with my previous arguments about reducing the emphasis on the vocational and selective aspects of school and stressing instead the civic (properly defined) and the aesthetic.

2   Multi-ethnic Curricula

The problem of a curriculum for ethnic minorities is similar only in some respects. The objection here might be that it is inappropriate to prescribe a curriculum for a cultural minority based on the culture of the dominant native group. Why should it be assumed that a curriculum derived from an alien culture is acceptable to or appropriate for an immigrant community? The answer is, in one respect, simple. The task of curriculum planning should be concerned with what young people need to know, understand or experience in order to participate effectively in a given society. In the UK, for example, whether a child is black or white, Catholic or Protestant, working-class or middle-class, he or she will be better equipped if he knows something of the history of the UK, of science, mathematics and technology. Unless as adults they are to be excluded from participation and decision-making, pupils will need to master certain ideas and concepts. To become educated they also need to acquire a variety of leisure-time pursuits – but these are less central to the core curriculum, that is, much more variety is desirable.

In fact, it is precisely because the USA, the UK and Australia are multicultural societies that we need to be concerned with questions of the common culture and the common curriculum. If there were no cultural diversity there would be less dispute about curriculum content.

Outside the common curriculum there should be plenty of opportunity for cultural differences to be celebrated – in art, music, dance, as well as religious and social values. But these must be in addition to, not instead of, a common curriculum. We should also be very wary of projects which attempt to increase the respect for, and self-respect of, ethnic minorities, but deal only with cultural artefacts rather than belief systems and thought processes. It is all too easy to get stuck at the level of basket-work and folk dancing. The proper balance between a common curriculum and cultural diversity at the periphery is another question. This is essentially a matter of detail, but a very important detail.

Another word of warning is also necessary. I have been talking of the education of ethnic minorities whose members have taken a conscious choice to move into a given society (for example, West Indians in the UK; Greek immigrants in Australia). The common curriculum must be designed to enable their children to become not just members, but participant members of a society. The case may well be very different for ethnic minorities who have no wish to 'join' the mainstream society or to participate in its culture. Some Indian communities in Canada and some aborigines in Australia may well be in that category. In such cases, the policy problems are totally different from those of planning a common curriculum.

Summary

I have attempted to answer two kinds of criticism of the idea of a common curriculum based on common culture. The common curriculum does *not* rest upon assumptions about cultural uniformity and consensus; quite the opposite – a common curriculum is a means of coping with cultural diversity in a positive way. One of the functions of a school is to help the young to equip themselves with the knowledge necessary for participation in adult society. Cultural analysis enables those concerned with curriculum planning to make a selection from culture which will enable *all* young people to understand and, if necessary, to change the society in which they live.

NOTE

1 Harold Entwistle also argues this case in his *Class, Culture and Education* (1978). See also his study of *Antonio Gramsci* (1979). Both writers argue against the folly of a different curriculum which would be particularly relevant to working-class pupils. This would be to deprive them of the possibility of access to knowledge and power. Gramsci, for example, argues that working-class 'commonsense'

often obscures the power relations in society, encourages fatalism and a capacity for 'putting up' with things as they are rather than wanting to change them.

10 The Open Curriculum and its Enemies

Instead of encouraging the student to devote himself to his studies for the sake of studying, instead of encouraging in him a real love for his subject and for enquiry, he is encouraged to study for the sake of his personal career – he is led to acquire only such knowledge as is serviceable in getting him over the hurdles which he must clear for the sake of his advancement . . . I do not know a better argument for an optimistic view of mankind, no better proof of their indestructible love for truth and decency . . . than the fact that this devastating system of education has not utterly ruined them.

Karl Popper*

This book began with a discussion of the relation between ideology and education, and I want – by way of conclusion – to return to that theme.

Any discussion of education is political and ideological. It is, however, a mistake to assume that there is always a direct link between a particular educational practice or innovation, and one specific political or ideological viewpoint. Reality is usually more complex. Thus to attribute the rise of elementary education in nineteenth-century England simply to the need for industrialists to have an adequate supply of literated and obedient manpower would be too naïve. Other important ideological motives were also involved; a genuinely religious desire to save souls (which must be distinguished from cynical or hypocritical exploitation of religious values); a genuinely humanitarian concern for the poor (as well as a fear of revolution).

Underlying all those attitudes are perhaps two basic and contrasting educational ideologies, which although rarely existing in a pure form, must for the sake of analysis, be identified. The first set

* (1945) *The Open Society and Its Enemies*.

of values might be described as 'education as liberation'. It is based partly on the assumption that human beings are not entirely evil and can be improved by education in such a way as to enrich their lives both as individuals and as members of the society. This is related to 'open education' in two senses: it is based on the assumption that education ought to be open-ended in terms of subject matter and duration – there is no final goal, only a series of valuable journeys; it is open also in terms of accessibility to all who wish to learn or can be encouraged to learn.

The second kind of educational ideology might be called 'education as social control'. It is based on fear: fear of individuals not conforming to social norms; fear of political or social revolution; fear of innovation or loss of traditions; fear of uncertainty. For those with such attitudes, education may be a means of controlling opportunities rather than encouraging them; they will be concerned with standards and correct answers. The behavioural objective approach to education has obvious appeal to them. So have all forms of tests and examinations. Schooling is concerned with preparation for the world of work and what has been referred to by Raymond Callahan as 'the cult of efficiency'.

Thus I am suggesting that educational ideologies are related to deep-rooted personality factors as well as to 'political' beliefs. Over-riding both ideologies, however, is the need for a society to pass on fundamental aspects of culture, including beliefs and values. Clearly no complete consensus is possible, given these two very different 'ideal type' ideologies, but a common policy has to be worked out within any society. One of the constraints is itself political: if our claim to be a democratic society is to be taken seriously, then certain social and political – as well as educational – consequences have to follow. For example, in a democracy, in the long run inherited privilege must be regarded as morally indefensible, and it will eventually be unthinkable for the children of the rich to inherit educational advantages. Perhaps future generations will look back on inherited wealth with much the same puzzlement as we now consider such feudal privileges as *droit de seigneur*! But that is to stray too far into the future. It is, however, possible to say that, given a commitment to democracy, then certain trends would seem to follow logically – even if rearguard actions are to be expected from time to time. 'Open', comprehensive schools with open common curricula (as defined in chapter 8) are among these necessary democratic features, in the long run. But truly 'open' education policies will involve reformed teacher/

pupil relations and better school organisation as well as reformed curricula. Schools generally still retain too much of the nineteenth century 'workhouse' concern for social control. Much more work is necessary to analyse and improve the internal cultural arrangements of schools. This is not, of course, to recommend the A. S. Neill 'Summerhill' approach: schools must be orderly without resembling prisons or nineteenth-century factories. It seems to me that at the moment in England many schools are, in fact, too noisy; but ways have to be found of establishing purposefulness without repressive control. There are many examples of primary and secondary schools which have succeeded in this respect, but the secret of 'transferability' has to be analysed and made available. This is part of the cultural analysis of schools yet to be undertaken in a serious way. It is clearly not enough to suggest in the manner of HMI *Ten Good Schools* that good schools need very good head teachers. If a structure depends on a single individual, then the structure is a poor one.

The progress towards a more democratic and open system is in keeping with the general process of cultural change, but educational controversy will not disappear. It would be unwise to underestimate the difficulties and problems such as those described by Paul Willis (1977) of alienated working-class boys for whom education appeared to be almost totally irrelevant. Overcoming that kind of tradition will be enormously difficult, but neither should such problems be exaggerated. Most schools, even in urban inner city areas, are not 'blackboard jungles'.[1] It is, however, true that the problems of young people growing up in urban, industrialised areas have probably been seriously underestimated and neglected.

Whilst in a plural society some conflict will be inevitable, cultural analysis can at least clarify the issues and distinguish between productive and unproductive tensions within the system. In this book, I have been particularly concerned to use cultural analysis to indicate deficiencies in existing curricula. I would stress once again that this is only part of the solution, but it is an important part.

In particular, I would want to conclude by stressing a number of cultural features which should help improve curriculum planning. First, I have identified a number of serious 'gaps' in school curricula, especially political and moral education; second, there is an over-emphasis on the instrumental aspects of schooling – particularly a narrow view of the link between school and work;

third, there is a corresponding neglect of expressive aspects of education – especially aesthetic and social development; fourth, there is a shameful curricular neglect of the majority of pupils not seen as destined for higher education or 'white collar' employment. This is, of course, linked with an extremely damaging and antiquated examination system at 16+ which encourages teachers and pupils to think of the majority of the older, secondary age-group as failures. A more 'open' system based on a common culture curriculum would have to counteract all those powerfully entrenched traditional features.

Looking at the problem from the opposite point of view, the enemies of the 'open' curriculum might be identified as follows: first, those who see merit in the present cafeteria curriculum either for reasons of segregating the 'able' or for mistaken attachment to the appearance, but not the reality, of 'choice' – the kind of choice which is the enemy of true freedom. Associated with the false freedom of choice is the neglect of planning, as Mannheim (1940) warned. We must plan to have a balanced curriculum available for all pupils. Compulsion should be seen as unnecessary, but more than mere accessibility will be required – teachers must learn to persuade convincingly rather than manipulate the young into following a worthwhile curriculum. A second important enemy is the narrowly utilitarian attitude to education and the curriculum. If schooling is identified with preparation for work, not only does this narrow and distort the teachers' vision, but it will alienate the majority of pupils, as Popper (1945) warned in the immediate post-war period. This does not mean that the world of work should be ignored, merely that it must be kept in perspective. There are good arguments for suggesting that more attention should be given to work as an aspect of culture, but without schooling being dominated by the needs of employers.

Another enemy is the narrow, closed view of education represented by the behavioural objectives school of curriculum planning, APU testing and a one-way bureaucratic system of accountability. The more the educational system is associated with short-term goals, check lists and testing, the more difficult it is for the curriculum to be open, and for teachers to become truly professional educators rather than child-minders.

Finally, in England, a very important enemy is the whole of the examination industry. 16+ examinations are not only means of perpetuating a segregated system of secondary schooling, they also dominate and distort all discussions of secondary curriculum reform. It might be argued that the demise of the Schools Council was caused directly by the fact that it had to fight a battle over examinations for the whole of its existence when it should have been concerned with curriculum reform. In England, it is still true to say that the 'evaluation tail wags the curriculum dog'.

Much more detailed work is desirable at the national level, but even more important and urgent is the study of the school from the same cultural analysis perspective. What all schools need in terms of curriculum guidelines is now reasonably clear, and the procedures for working on the details are also available. But what remains to be analysed is the school as a social network so that the problem of teacher/pupil relations and the school as a humane, social system can also be reformed.

NOTE

1 HMI Secondary School Survey (1979) stated that most schools are reasonably orderly. Nevertheless too many schools are still dreary, unexciting places for young people – and their teachers.

Bibliography

ACKERMAN, B. A. (1980) *Social Justice in the Liberal State*. New Haven, Conn.: Yale University Press.

ADELMAN, C., JENKINS, D. and KEMMIS, S. (1976) 'Rethinking Case Study: Notes from the Second Cambridge Conference', *Cambridge Journal of Education*, Vol. 6, No. 3.

ARNOLD, M. (1869) *Culture and Anarchy*. Cambridge: Cambridge University Press.

ATKIN, J. M. (1979) 'Educational Accountability in the United States', *Educational Analysis*, Vol. 1, No. 1, 5–21.

AULD, R. (1976) *William Tyndale Junior and Infant Schools Public Enquiry*. London: Inner London Education Authority.

BAGLEY, W. L. (1907) *Classroom Management*. New York: Macmillan.

BANTOCK, G. (1971) 'Towards a theory of Popular Education' in GOLBY, M. *et al.* (1975) *Curriculum Design*. London: Croom Helm.

BARNES, D. *et al.* (1969) *Language, the Learner and the School*. Harmondsworth: Penguin.

BECHER, A. (1979) 'Self-accounting, Evaluation and Accountability', *Educational Analysis*, Vol. 1, No. 1, 63–6.

BECHER, A. and MACLURE, S. (1978) *The Politics of Curriculum Change*. London: Hutchinson.

BECHER, A., ERAUT, M. and KNIGHT, J. (1981) *Politics for Educational Accountability*. London: Heinemann.

BENEDICT, R. (1934) *Patterns of Culture*. Various editions.

BENNETT, N. (ed.) (1976) *Teaching Styles and Pupil Progress*. London: Open Books.

BERNSTEIN, B. (1975) *Class, Codes and Control*, Vol. III. London: Routledge and Kegan Paul.

BOARD OF EDUCATION (1938) *Report of the Consultative Committee on Secondary Education with Special Reference to Grammar Schools and Technical High Schools* (The Spens Report). London: HMSO.

BOBBITT, F. (1912) *The Elimination of Waste in Education*. Boston, Mass.: Houghton Mifflin.

BOBBITT, F. (1918) *The Curriculum*. Boston, Mass.: Houghton Mifflin.

BOBBITT, F. (1924) *How to Make a Curriculum*. Boston, Mass.: Houghton Mifflin.

BRUNER, J. (1960) *The Process of Education*. Cambridge, Mass.: Harvard University Press.

BRUNER, J. (1966) *Towards a Theory of Instruction*. Cambridge, Mass.: Harvard University Press.

BUTTON, L. (1981, 1982) *Group Tutoring for the Form Teacher: 1 Lower Secondary School, 2 Upper Secondary School*. London: Hodder & Stoughton.

CALLAHAN, R. E. (1962) *Education and the Cult of Efficiency*. Chicago, Ill.: University of Chicago Press.

CATTELL, R. B. (1949) 'The Dimensions of Culture Patterns by Factorization of National Characters', *Abnormal Social Psychology*, 44, 443–69.

CENTRAL ADVISORY COUNCIL FOR EDUCATION (CACE) (1959) *15 to 18* (The Crowther Report). London: HMSO.

CENTRAL ADVISORY COUNCIL FOR EDUCATION (CACE) (1963) *Children and Their Primary Schools* (The Plowden Report). London: HMSO.

CHOMSKY, N. (1959) Review of B. F. Skinner 'Verbal Behaviour' in *Language*, 35, 26–8. Reprinted in FODOR, J. A. and KATZ, J. J. (1965) *The Structure of Language*. Hemel Hempstead: Prentice-Hall.

CLARKE, SIR FRED (1943) *Education and Social Change*. London: Sheldon Press.

CRICK, B. and PORTER, A. (eds) (1979) *Political Education and the Programme for Political Literacy*. Harlow: Longman.

CRONBACH, L. J. (1963) 'Evaluation for Course Improvement' in HEATH, R. (ed.) *New Curricula*. London: Harper and Row.

DEARDEN, R. F. (1968) *Philosophy of Primary School Education*. London: Routledge and Kegan Paul.

DEARDEN, R. F. (1981) 'Balance and Coherence', *Cambridge Journal of Education*, Vol 11, No. 2.

DEARDEN, R. F., HIRST, P. H. and PETERS, R. S. (eds) (1972) *Education and the Development of Reason*. London: Routledge and Kegan Paul.

DEPARTMENT OF EDUCATION AND SCIENCE (1975) *A Language for Life* (The Bullock Report). London: HMSO.

DEPARTMENT OF EDUCATION AND SCIENCE (1977) *A New Partnership for Our Schools* (The Taylor Report). London: HMSO.

DEPARTMENT OF EDUCATION AND SCIENCE (1977) 'Ten Good Schools' (*Matters for Discussion*, No. 1). London: HMSO.

DEPARTMENT OF EDUCATION AND SCIENCE (1977) *Curriculum 11–16*. London: HMSO.

DEPARTMENT OF EDUCATION AND SCIENCE (1977) *Education in Schools: A Consultative Document* (Green Paper). London: HMSO.

DEPARTMENT OF EDUCATION AND SCIENCE (1978) *A Survey of Primary Education*. London: HMSO.

DEPARTMENT OF EDUCATION AND SCIENCE (1979) *Aspects of Secondary*

Education in England (The Secondary School Survey). London: HMSO.

DEPARTMENT OF EDUCATION AND SCIENCE (1979) *A Framework for the School Curriculum*. London: HMSO.

DEPARTMENT OF EDUCATION AND SCIENCE (1980) *A View of the Curriculum*. London: HMSO.

DEPARTMENT OF EDUCATION AND SCIENCE (1981) *The Secondary Curriculum 11–16: A Report on Progress*. London: HMSO.

DEPARTMENT OF EDUCATION AND SCIENCE (1982) *Technology in Schools*. London: HMSO.

DWORKIN, R. (1977) *Taking Rights Seriously*. London: Duckworth.

EISNER, E. W. (1969) 'Instructional and Expressive Educational Objectives' in POPHAM, W. J. *et al*. (eds) *Instructional Objectives*. Chicago, Ill.: Rand McNally.

EISNER, E. W. (ed.) (1971) *Confronting Curriculum Reform*. Boston, Mass.: Little, Brown.

EISNER, E. W. (1975) 'The Perceptive Eye: Towards the Reformation of Educational Evaluation.' Paper prepared for a meeting of the American Educational Research Association (AERA), Washington, D.C.

ELIOT, T. S. (1948) *Notes Towards a Definition of Culture*. London: Faber.

ELLIOTT, J. and ADELMAN, C. (eds) (1975) *Classroom Action Research*. Cambridge: Ford Teaching Project.

ELLIOTT, J. and ADELMAN, C. (eds) (1975) *Eliciting Pupils' Accounts in the Classroom*. Cambridge: Ford Teaching Project.

ELLIOTT, J. and ADELMAN, C. (eds) (1975) *Innovation Process in the Classroom*. Cambridge: Ford Teaching Project.

ELLIOTT, J. and ADELMAN, C. (eds) (1975) *Language and Logic of Informal Teaching*. Cambridge: Ford Teaching Project.

ELLIOTT, J and HURLIN, T. (eds) (1975) *Self-Monitoring Questioning Strategies*. Cambridge: Ford Teaching Project.

ELLIOTT, J. and PARTINGTON, D. (eds) (1975) *Three Points of View in the Classroom: Generating Hypotheses from Classroom Observations, Recordings and Interviews*. Cambridge: Ford Teaching Project.

ENTWISTLE, H. (1978) *Class, Culture and Education*. London: Routledge and Kegan Paul.

ENTWISTLE, H. (1979) *Antonio Gramsci*. London: Routledge and Kegan Paul.

ERAUT, M. (1981) 'Accountability and Evaluation' in SIMON, B. and TAYLOR, W. (eds) (1981) *Education in the Eighties*. London: Batsford.

FLOUD, J. E. (1962) 'Teaching in the Affluent Society', *British Journal of Sociology*, Vol. 13, 299–308.

FLOUD, J. E., HALSEY, A. H. and MARTIN, F. M. (1956) *Social Class and Educational Opportunity*. London: Heinemann.

FORD, J. (1968) *Social Class and the Comprehensive School*. London: Routledge and Kegan Paul.

GEERTZ, C. (1975) *The Interpretation of Cultures*. New York: Basic Books.

GLASS, D. V. (1954) *Social Mobility in Britain*. London: Routledge and Kegan Paul.

GOLBY, M. *et al.* (eds) (1975) *Curriculum Design*. London: Croom Helm.

GOODENOUGH, W. H. (1961) 'Comment on Cultural Evolution', *Daedalus*, 90, 514–33.

GRAMSCI, A. (1971) *Selections from Prison Notebooks*. London: Lawrence and Wishart.

GRAY, J. (1981) 'From Policy to Practice – Some Problems and Paradoxes of Egalitarian Reform' in SIMON, B. and TAYLOR, W. (eds) (1981) *Education in the Eighties: The Central Issues*. London: Batsford.

GULBENKIAN FOUNDATION (1982) *The Arts in Schools*. Calouste Gulbenkian Foundation.

HAMILTON, D. *et al.* (eds) (1977) *Beyond the Numbers Game*. London: Macmillan.

HER MAJESTY'S INSPECTORS, see under DEPARTMENT OF EDUCATION AND SCIENCE.

HIRST, P. (1975) *Knowledge and Curriculum*. London: Routledge and Kegan Paul.

HOGGART, R. (1960) *Uses of Literacy*. Harmondsworth: Penguin.

HOLT, M. (1981) *Evaluating the Evaluators*. London: Hodder and Stoughton.

HOUSE, E. (1973) *School Evaluation*. Berkeley, Calif.: McCutchan.

HOUSE, E. (1975) 'Accountability in the USA', *Cambridge Journal of Education*, Vol. 5, No. 2.

HOUSE, E. (1978) 'An American View of British Accountability' in BECHER, A. and MACLURE, S. (eds) (1978).

HOUSE, E., RIVERS, L. and STUFFLEBEAM, D. (1974) *An Assessment of the Michigan Accountability System*. Washington, D.C.: National Education Association.

HURMAN, A. (1979) *A Charter for Choice*. Windsor: NFER.

KAY, B. (1975) 'Monitoring School Performance', *Trends in Education*. London: HMSO.

KEESING, R. M. and KEESING, F. M. (1971) *New Perspectives in Cultural Anthropology*. New York: Holt, Rinehart and Winston.

KERR, J. F. (ed.) (1968) *Changing the Curriculum*. London: University of London Press Ltd.

KING, E. J. (1979) *Other Schools and Ours*. New York: Holt, Rinehart and Winston.

KLIEBARD, H. M. (1970) 'The Tyler Rationale', *School Review*, Vol. 78, 259.

KLUCKHOHN, C. (1949) *Mirror for Man*. New York: Whittlesey House.

KLUCKHOHN, C. (1951) 'Values and Value-explorations in the Theory of Action: an Exploration in Definition and Classification' in PARSONS,

T. and SHILS, E. T. (eds) *Towards a General Theory of Action*. Cambridge, Mass.: Harvard University Press.

KLUCKHOHN, F. and STRODTBECK, F. L. (1961) *Variations in Value Orientations*. Evanston, Ill.: Row, Peterson.

KOGAN, M. (1978) *The Politics of Educational Change*. London: Collins/Fontana.

KOHLBERG, L. (1964) 'Development of Moral Character and Moral Ideology' in HOFFMAN, M. L. and HOFFMAN, L. W. (eds) *Review of Child Development Research*, Vol. 1. Beverly Hills, Calif.: Sage.

LACEY, C. and LAWTON, D. (1981) *Issues in Evaluation and Accountability*. London: Methuen.

LAUWERYS, J. H. (ed.) (1945) *The Content of Education*. London: Council for Curriculum Reform/University of London Press Ltd.

LAWTON, D. (1973) *Social Change, Educational Theory and Curriculum Planning*. London: Hodder and Stoughton.

LAWTON, D. (1975) *Class, Culture and the Curriculum*. London: Routledge and Kegan Paul.

LAWTON, D. (1977) *Education and Social Justice*. Beverly Hills, Calif.: Sage.

LAWTON, D. (1979, 2nd ed.) *Investigating Society*. London: Hodder and Stoughton.

LAWTON, D. (1980) *The Politics of the School Curriculum*. London: Routledge and Kegan Paul.

LAWTON, D. (1981) *An Introduction to Teaching and Learning*. London: Hodder and Stoughton.

LAWTON, D. and DUFOUR, B. (1973) *The New Social Studies*. London: Heinemann.

LEE, D. (1960) *Enduring Human Values* (mimeo) California Association for Nursery Education quoted by WESTBY-GIBSON, D. (1965) in *Social Perspectives on Education*. New York: Wiley.

LESSINGER, L. M. (1971) 'Accountability for Results' in LESSINGER and TYLER (1971).

LESSINGER, L. M. and TYLER, R. W. (1971) *Accountability in Education*. Washington, Ohio: C. A. Jones.

LEVI-STRAUSS, C. (1966) *The Savage Mind*. London: Heinemann.

LINTON, R. (ed.) (1940) *Acculturation*. New York: Appleton-Century-Crofts.

MACDONALD, B. (1976) 'Accountability, Standards and the Process of Schooling' in BECHER, A. and MACLURE, S. (eds) (1978).

MacKENZIE, R. F. (1970) *State School*. Harmondsworth: Penguin.

MACLURE, S. (1978) 'Background to the Accountability Debate' in BECHER, A. and MACLURE, S. (eds) *Accountability in Education*. Windsor: NFER.

McPHAIL, P., UNGOED-THOMAS, J. R. and CHAPMAN, H. (1972) *Moral Education in the Secondary School*. Harlow: Longman.

MACCIA, E. S. (1965) *Methodological Considerations in Curriculum Theory Building*. Chicago, Ill.: ASCD.

MAGER, R. F. (1962) *Preparing Objectives for Programmed Instruction*. San Francisco, Calif.: Fearon.

MANNHEIM, K. (1940) *Man and Society in an Age of Reconstruction*. London: Routledge and Kegan Paul.

MANZER, R. A. (1970) *Teachers and Politics*. Manchester: Manchester University Press.

MAY, P. R. (1971) *Moral Education in Schools*. London: Methuen.

MURDOCK, G. P. (1949) *Social Structure*. New York: Macmillan (Free Press paperback, 1965).

MUSGRAVE, P. W. (ed.) (1970) *Sociology, History and Education*. London: Methuen.

MUSGROVE, F. (1979) *School and the Social Order*. New York: Wiley.

NEILL, A. S. (1926) *The Problem Child*. London: Herbert Jenkins.

O'HEAR, A. (1981) *Education, Society and Human Nature*. London: Routledge and Kegan Paul.

OZOLINS, U. (1979) 'Lawton's "Refutation" of a Working Class Curriculum', *Melbourne Working Papers*. Melbourne, Victoria: University of Melbourne.

PALMER, I. (1979) *Matthew Arnold: Culture, Society and Education*. Melbourne, Victoria: Macmillan.

PARLETT, M. and HAMILTON, D. (1972) 'Evaluation as Illumination', in TAWNEY, D. (1976) *Curriculum Evaluation Today*. London: Macmillan.

PETERS, R. S. (1966) *Ethics and Education*. London: Allen and Unwin.

PETERS, R. S. (ed.) (1968) *Perspectives on Plowden*. London: Routledge and Kegan Paul.

PEVSNER, N. (1956) *The Englishness of English Art*. Harmondsworth: Penguin.

PHENIX, P. H. (1964) *Realms of Meaning*. London: McGraw-Hill.

POPHAM, W. J. (1969) 'Objectives and Instruction' in POPHAM, W. J. *et al.* (eds) *Instructional Objectives*. Chicago, Ill.: AERA/Rand McNally.

POPPER, K. R. (1945) *The Open Society and Its Enemies*. London: Routledge and Kegan Paul.

PRING, R. (1972) 'Knowledge out of Control', *Education for Teaching*, Autumn.

PRING, R. (1976) *Knowledge and Schooling*. London: Open Books.

PRING, R. (1982) 'Personal and Social Development', *Cambridge Journal of Education*, Vol. 12, No. 1, 3–14.

RAWLS, J. (1972) *A Theory of Justice*. London: Oxford University Press.

REID, M. *et al.* (1974) *A Matter of Choice*. Windsor: NFER.

REID, W. (1978) *Thinking About the Curriculum*. London: Routledge and Kegan Paul.

REYNOLDS, J. and SKILBECK, M. (1976) *Culture and the Classroom*. London: Open Books.

ROBINS, D. and COHEN, P. (1978) *Knuckle Sandwich*. Harmondsworth: Penguin.

RODERICK, G. and STEVENS, M. (1981) *Where Did We Go Wrong? Industry, Education and Economy of Victorian England*. London: Falmer.

RUTTER, M. *et al.* (1979) *Fifteen Thousand Hours*. London: Open Books.

SCHOOLS COUNCIL (1973) *Evaluation in Curriculum Development: Twelve Case Studies*. London: Macmillan.

SCHOOLS COUNCIL (1975) Working Paper 53, *The Whole Curriculum 13–16*. London: Schools Council/Evans.

SCHOOLS COUNCIL (1975) Working Paper 55, *The Curriculum in the Middle Years*. London: Schools Council/Evans.

SHIPMAN, M. (1974) *Inside a Curriculum Project*. London: Methuen.

SIMON, B. and TAYLOR, W. (eds) (1981) *Education in the Eighties*. London: Batsford.

SIMONS, H. (1980) *Towards a Science of the Singular*. Norwich: University of East Anglia.

SKILBECK, M. (1976) 'Ideologies and Values', Unit 3 of Course E203, *Curriculum Design and Development*. Milton Keynes: Open University.

SKINNER, B. F. (1968) *The Technology of Teaching*. New York: Appleton-Century-Crofts.

SOCKETT, H. (ed.) (1980) *Accountability in the English Educational System*. London: Hodder and Stoughton.

STAKE, R. (1974) *Program Evaluation Particularly Responsive Education*. Chicago, Ill.: Centre for Instructional Research and Curriculum Evaluation, University of Illinois.

STENHOUSE, L. (1970) 'Some Limitations of the Use of Objectives in Curriculum Research and Planning', *Paedagogica Europaea*, Vol. 6, 73–83.

STENHOUSE, L. (1975) *An Introduction to Curriculum Research and Development*. London: Heinemann.

STRADLING, R. (1977) *The Political Awareness of the Young School Leaver*. London: Hansard Society.

STUBBS, M. (1976) *Language, Schools and Classrooms*. London: Methuen.

TABA, H. (1962) *Curriculum Development*. New York: Harcourt, Brace and World.

TANNER, D. and TANNER, L. (1975) *Curriculum Development*. London: Macmillan.

TAWNEY, R. H. (1926) *Religion and the Rise of Capitalism*. London: Penguin, 1938.

TAWNEY, R. H. (1931) *Equality*. London: Allen and Unwin, 1964.

THOMPSON, E. P. (1968) *The Making of the English Working Class*. Harmondsworth: Penguin.

TYLER, R. W. (1949) *Basic Principles of Curriculum and Instruction*. Chicago, Ill.: University of Chicago Press.

TYLER, R. W. (1973) 'The Father of Behavioural Objectives Criticises Them', *Phi Delta Kappan*, Vol. 55, 57.

TYLOR, E. B. (1871) *Primitive Culture*. London: Murray.

WEINER, M. J. (1981) *English Culture and the Decline of the Industrial Spirit*. Cambridge: Cambridge University Press.

WHEELER, D. K. (1967) *Curriculum Process*. London: University of London Press Ltd.

WHITE, J. P. (1973) *Towards a Compulsory Curriculum*. London: Routledge and Kegan Paul.

WHITEHEAD, D. (1979) *Handbook for Economics Teachers*. London: Heinemann.

WILLIAMS, R. (1958) *Culture and Society*. Harmondsworth: Penguin.

WILLIAMS, R. (1961) *The Long Revolution*. Harmondsworth: Penguin.

WILLIAMS, R. (1976) *Keywords*. London: Collins/Fontana.

WILLIAMS, R. (1981) *Culture*. London: Collins/Fontana.

WILLIS, P. (1977) *Learning to Labour*. Farnborough: Saxon House.

WILSON, J. (1969) *Moral Education and the Curriculum*. Oxford: Pergamon.

WILSON, J. (1971) *Education in Religion and the Emotions*. London: Heinemann.

YOUNG, M. (1958) *The Rise of the Meritocracy*. London: Thames and Hudson.

YOUNG, M. F. D. (ed.) (1971) *Knowledge and Control*. New York: Collier-Macmillan.

Index